Here's what the critics say about Frommer's:

"Amazingly easy to use. Very portable, very complete."

—*Booklist*

♦

"The only mainstream guide to list specific prices. The Walter Cronkite of guidebooks—with all that implies."

—*Travel & Leisure*

PORTABLE

Phoenix & Scottsdale

1st Edition

by Karl Samson

with Jane Aukshunas

HUNGRY MINDS, INC.

New York, NY • Cleveland, OH • Indianapolis, IN

Chicago, IL • Foster City, CA • San Francisco, CA

About the Authors

Karl Samson and **Jane Aukshunas,** husband-and-wife travel-writing team, find that the sunny winter skies of the Arizona desert are the perfect antidote to the dreary winters of their Pacific Northwest home. Each winter, they flee the rain to explore Arizona's deserts, mountains, cities, and small towns. Summers find the team researching their other books, including *Frommer's Washington*, *Frommer's Oregon*, and *Frommer's Seattle & Portland.*

Published By:

HUNGRY MINDS, INC.

909 Third Avenue
New York, NY 10022
www.frommers.com

ISBN 0-7645-6451-X
ISSN 1532-9895

Editor: Myka Carroll
Production Editor: Donna Wright
Photo Editor: Richard Fox
Design by Michele Laseau
Cartographer: John Decamillis
Production by Hungry Minds Indianapolis Production Services
Cover Photo: Golfing at The Boulders resort in Carefree, AZ

Special Sales

For general information on Hungry Minds' products and services please contact our Customer Care department; within the U.S. at 800-762-2974, outside the U.S. at 317-572-3993 or fax 317-572-4002. For sales inquiries and reseller information, including discounts, bulk sales, customized editions, and premium sales, please contact our Customer Care department at 800-434-3422.

Manufactured in the United States of America

5 4 3 2 1

Contents

List of Maps

An Invitation to the Reader

In researching this book we have discovered many wonderful places—hotels, restaurants, shops, and more. We're sure you'll find others. Please tell us about them, so that we can share the information with your fellow travelers in upcoming editions. If you were disappointed with a recommendation, we'd love to know that, too. Please write to:

Frommer's Portable Phoenix & Scottsdale, 1st Edition
Hungry Minds, Inc.
909 Third Avenue, 20th Floor
New York, NY 10022

An Additional Note

Please be advised that travel information is subject to change at any time, and this is especially true of prices. We therefore suggest that you write or call ahead for confirmation when making your travel plans. The authors, editors, and publishers cannot be held responsible for the experiences of readers while traveling. Your safety is important to us, however, so we encourage you to stay alert and be aware of your surroundings. Keep a close eye on cameras, purses, and wallets, all favorite targets of thieves and pickpockets.

What the Symbols Mean

✪ Frommer's Favorites

Our favorite places and experiences—outstanding for quality, value, or both.

The following abbreviations are used for credit cards:

AE American Express
CB Carte Blanche
DC Diners Club
DISC Discover
ER EnRoute
EC Eurocard
JCB Japan Credit Bank
MC MasterCard
V Visa

Find Frommer's Online

www.frommers.com offers up-to-the-minute listings on almost 200 cities around the globe—including the latest bargains and candid, personal articles updated daily by Arthur Frommer himself. No other Web site offers such comprehensive and timely coverage of the world of travel.

1

The Best of Phoenix & Scottsdale

We've chosen what we feel is the very best Phoenix, Scottsdale, and the Valley of the Sun have to offer—the places and experiences you won't want to miss. Although the places and activities listed here are written up in more detail elsewhere in this book, this chapter should give you an overview of the highlights and get you started on planning your trip.

1 Frommer's Favorite Experiences in Phoenix, Scottsdale & the Valley of the Sun

- **Lounging by the Pool.** Nothing is more relaxing than lounging by one of the spectacular pools and gazing up at the desert mountains from a world-class Valley of the Sun resort. See chapter 4.
- **Having Dinner with a View.** There's something bewitching about gazing down at the twinkling lights of the city while enjoying a delicious meal at one of the area's few hillside restaurants. See chapter 5.
- **Attending a Spring Training Baseball Game.** Get a head start on all your fellow baseball fans by going to a spring-training game while you're in Phoenix. Just be sure to book your hotel well in advance; these games are the biggest thing going in the valley each spring. See chapter 6.
- **Communing with Cacti at the Desert Botanical Garden.** There's no better place to learn about the plants of Arizona's Sonoran Desert and the many other deserts of the world. Displays at this Phoenix botanical garden explain plant adaptations and how indigenous tribes once used many of this region's wild plants. See chapter 6.
- **Gallery-Hopping on the Scottsdale Art Walk.** Thursday evenings from October to May, both dilettantes and connoisseurs turn out to visit the nearly 60 art galleries in downtown

Scottsdale, many of which have artists on hand and provide complimentary refreshments. See chapter 6.

- **Hiking Camelback Mountain or Squaw Peak.** For many Phoenicians the trail to the top of Camelback Mountain is a ritual, a Phoenix institution. Both trails are steep climbs, but the views from up top are superb. Bring water and start early in the morning if it's going to be a hot day. See chapter 6.
- **Mountain Biking in South Mountain or Papago Park.** The trails of these two desert parks are ideal for mountain biking, and whether you're a novice making your first foray onto the dirt or a budding downhill racer, you'll find miles of riding that are just your speed. See chapter 6.
- **Spending the Day at a Spa.** When it comes to stress relief, there's nothing like a massage or an herbal wrap. The chance to lie back and do nothing at all is something few of us take the time for anymore, so a day at the spa just might be the best thing you can do for yourself on vacation. See chapter 6.
- **Catching a Performance by Estéban.** Scottsdale's best and most popular lounge act is a Spanish guitarist who goes by the name of Estéban. The high-energy music pulls in huge crowds, and the lounge walls are usually thrown open to the night air. Order a cocktail or some dessert and you've got a great, relatively cheap night out. See chapter 7.
- **Driving the Apache Trail.** Much of this winding road, which passes just north of the Superstition Mountains, is unpaved and follows a rugged route once ridden by Apaches. This is some of the most remote country you'll find in the Phoenix area, with far-reaching desert vistas and lots to see and do along the way. See chapter 8.
- **Savoring the Scenery at the Boyce Thompson Southwestern Arboretum.** Located just outside the town of Superior, this was the nation's first botanical garden established in a desert environment. It's set in a small canyon framed by cliffs, with desert plantings from all over the world—a fascinating place for an educational stroll in the desert. See chapter 8.
- **Seeing Rare Ancient Architecture at Casa Grande Ruins National Monument.** Unlike most of the other ruins in the state, this large and unusual structure is built of packed desert soil. Inscrutable and perplexing, Casa Grande seems to rise from nowhere. See chapter 8.

- **Taking the Family to Pioneer Arizona Living History Museum.** This museum features old buildings and costumed interpreters who show and tell what life was like for Arizona pioneers a century ago. See chapter 8.
- **Viewing Native American Ruins at Besh-Ba-Gowah Archaeological Park.** These reconstructed ruins have been set up to look the way they might have appeared 700 years ago, providing a bit more cultural context than other ruins in the state. See chapter 8.
- **Visiting Preserved Pueblos at Tonto National Monument.** Located east of Phoenix on the Apache Trail, this is one of the only easily accessible cliff dwellings in Arizona that you can still visit; you don't have to just observe from a distance. See chapter 8.

2 The Best Golf Courses

- **The Boulders South Course:** If you've ever seen a photo of someone teeing off beside a massive balancing rock and longed to play that same hole, then you've dreamed about playing The Boulders South Course. The South Course, a desert-style design by Jay Morrish, plays around and through the jumble of massive boulders for which the resort is named.
- **Gold Canyon Golf Resort:** Located east of Phoenix, Gold Canyon offers superb golfing at the foot of the Superstition Mountains. The second, third, and fourth holes on the Dinosaur Mountain Course are the truly memorable ones. They play across the foot of Dinosaur Mountain and are rated among the top holes in the state.
- **The Tournament Players Club (TPC) of Scottsdale:** If you've always dreamed of playing where the pros play, then you may want to schedule a visit to the Scottsdale Princess and book a tee time on the Stadium Course, which is the site of the PGA Tour's Phoenix Open.
- **Troon North Golf Club:** Designed by Tom Weiskopf and Jay Morrish, this semiprivate desert-style course in north Scottsdale is named for the famous Scottish links that overlook both the Firth of Forth and the Firth of Clyde—but that's where the similarities end. Troon North has two 18-hole courses, but the original, known as the Monument Course, is still the favorite.

- **The Wigwam Gold Course:** If you're a traditionalist who eschews those cactus- and rattlesnake-filled desert target courses, you'll want to beg, borrow, or steal a tee time on the Wigwam Resort's Gold Course. This 7,100-yard resort course west of Phoenix has long been an Arizona legend.

3 The Best Museums

- **Heard Museum:** This is one of the nation's premier museums and is devoted to Native American cultures. In addition to historical exhibits, a huge kachina collection, and an excellent museum store, there are annual exhibits of contemporary Native American art as well as dance performances and demonstrations of traditional skills.
- **Phoenix Art Museum:** This large art museum has acres of wall space and houses an outstanding collection of contemporary art, as well as a fascinating exhibit of miniature rooms.
- **Scottsdale Museum of Contemporary Art:** This is the Phoenix area's newest museum and is noteworthy as much for its bold contemporary architecture as for its wide variety of exhibits. Unlike the majority of area art galleries, this museum eschews cowboy art.

4 The Best Luxury Resorts

- **Arizona Biltmore Resort & Spa:** Combining discreet service and the architectural styling of Frank Lloyd Wright, the Arizona Biltmore has long been one of the most popular resorts in the state. Recent renovations have done much to improve the quality of the rooms, and a new pool is a big hit with families.
- **The Boulders:** Taking its name from the massive blocks of eroded granite scattered about the grounds of the resort, the Boulders is among the most exclusive and expensive resorts in the state. Pueblo architecture fits seamlessly with the landscape, and the golf course is the most breathtaking in Arizona.
- **The Fairmont Scottsdale Princess:** The Moorish styling and numerous fountains and waterfalls of this Scottsdale resort create a setting made for romance. Two superb restaurants—one serving Spanish cuisine and one serving gourmet Mexican fare—top it off.
- **Four Seasons Resort:** This new resort in north Scottsdale takes aim at the Valley's top-end luxury resorts and clearly hits the mark. The setting is dramatic, the accommodations are

spacious and luxurious, and the next-door neighbor is one of Arizona's top golf courses. The only drawback is the out-of-the-way location.

- **Hyatt Regency Scottsdale:** Contemporary desert architecture, dramatic landscaping, a water playground with its own beach, a staff that's always at the ready to assist you, several good restaurants that aren't overpriced, and even gondola rides—it all adds up to a lot of fun at one of the most smoothly run resorts in Arizona.
- **Marriott's Camelback Inn:** This is one of the few Scottsdale resorts that retains an old Arizona atmosphere without sacrificing comfort or modern conveniences. A full-service spa caters to those who crave pampering, while two golf courses (one recently renovated) provide plenty of challenging fairways and greens.
- **The Phoenician:** This Xanadu of the resort world is brimming with marble, crystal, and works of art, and with staff seemingly around every corner, the hotel offers its guests impeccable service. Two of the resort's dining rooms are among the finest restaurants in the city, and the views are hard to beat.
- **Royal Palms Hotel and Casitas:** With its Mediterranean styling and towering royal palms, this resort seems far removed from the glitz that prevails at most area resorts. The Royal Palms is a classic, perfect for romantic getaways, and the 14 designer showcase rooms are among the most dramatically styled rooms in the valley.

5 The Best Swimming Pools

- **Hyatt Regency:** This Scottsdale resort boasts a 10-pool, 2½-acre water playground complete with sand beach, waterfalls, sports pool, lap pool, adult pool, three-story waterslide, large whirlpool, and lots of waterfalls.
- **The Phoenician:** This system of seven pools is as impressive as the Hyatt's but has a much more sophisticated air about it. Waterfalls, a waterslide, play pools, a lap pool, and the crown jewel, a mother-of-pearl pool (actually opalescent tile), all add up to plenty of aquatic fun.
- **Pointe Hilton Squaw Peak Resort:** They don't just have a pool here; they have a River Ranch, with an artificial tubing river, a waterslide, and a waterfall pouring into the large, freeform main pool.

- **Pointe Hilton Tapatio Cliffs Resort:** The Falls, a slightly more adult-oriented pool complex than that at sister property Pointe Hilton Squaw Peak Resort, includes two lagoon pools, a 40-foot waterfall, a 130-foot waterslide, and rental cabanas.
- **Wyndham Buttes Resort:** A lush stream cascading over desert rocks seems to feed this freeform pool, a desert oasis fantasy world unmatched in the state. A narrow canal connects the two halves of the pool, and tucked in among the rocks are several whirlpools.

6 The Best Restaurants

- **Marquesa:** Located amid the Moorish architecture of the Scottsdale Princess resort, this Spanish restaurant specializes in Catalonian dishes. To dine here is to be totally immersed in a Mediterranean experience.
- **Mary Elaine's:** Located in Scottsdale's posh Phoenician resort, Mary Elaine's is where the elite dine in the Valley of the Sun. The menu focuses primarily on modern French flavors, although the chef doesn't limit himself.
- **T. Cook's:** Located within the Mediterranean cloisters of the Royal Palms Resort, T. Cook's is the most romantic restaurant in Phoenix. No other restaurant (with the possible exception of Marquesa) so thoroughly transports you to another place with both its decor and its cuisine.
- **Vincent Guerithault on Camelback:** The bold flavors of the Southwest are the focus of this ever-popular restaurant, where presentation is every bit as important as taste. Even if you aren't a fan of chilies, you'll find plenty of unusual flavor combinations to tempt your palate.

2

Planning Your Trip to Phoenix & Scottsdale

Time and again, Phoenix, a city named by an early settler from Britain, has lived up to its name. Like the phoenix of ancient mythology, Arizona's capital city rose from its own ashes—in this case, the ruins of an ancient Indian village. While it took nearly a century for this Phoenix to take flight, the city has risen from the dust of the desert to become one of the largest metropolitan areas in the country.

Although the city has had its economic ups and downs, the Phoenix metropolitan area, often referred to as the Valley of the Sun, is currently booming. The Camelback Corridor, which leads through north-central Phoenix, has become the corporate heartland of the city, and shiny glass office towers keep pushing up toward the desert sky. This burgeoning stretch of road has also become a corridor of upscale restaurants and shopping plazas, anchored by the Biltmore Fashion Park, the city's temple of high-end consumerism, and today, Phoenicians flock to this area both for work and play.

Even downtown Phoenix, long abandoned as simply a place to work, has taken on an entirely new look in the past few years and has positioned itself as the sports and events district for the Valley of the Sun. First came the America West Arena. Then more recently, the Arizona Diamondbacks baseball team took up residence in the Bank One Ballpark (BOB), one of the nation's only baseball stadiums with a retractable roof. So, on days when there are games or concerts scheduled at either of these venues, you can bet that downtown Phoenix will be a lively place. Additionally, the downtown area offers quite a few interesting attractions, including the world-class Arizona Science Center, the Phoenix Museum of History, historic Heritage Square (downtown's only remaining historic block), the Phoenix Museum of Art, and the Heard Museum.

Phoenix, Scottsdale & the Valley of the Sun

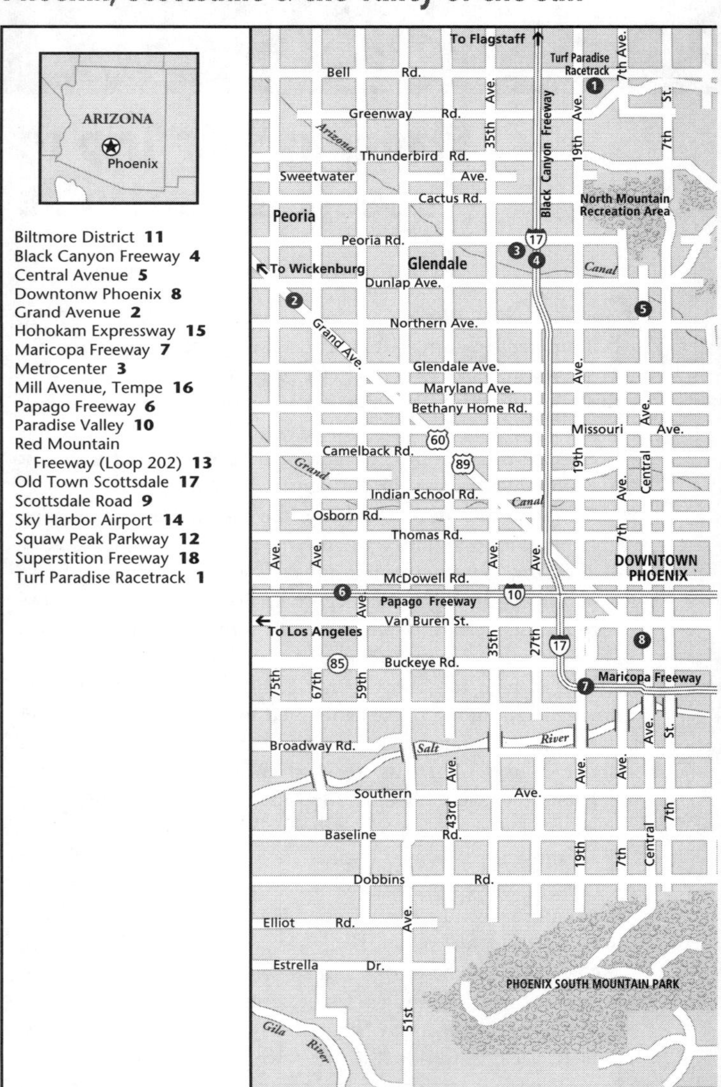

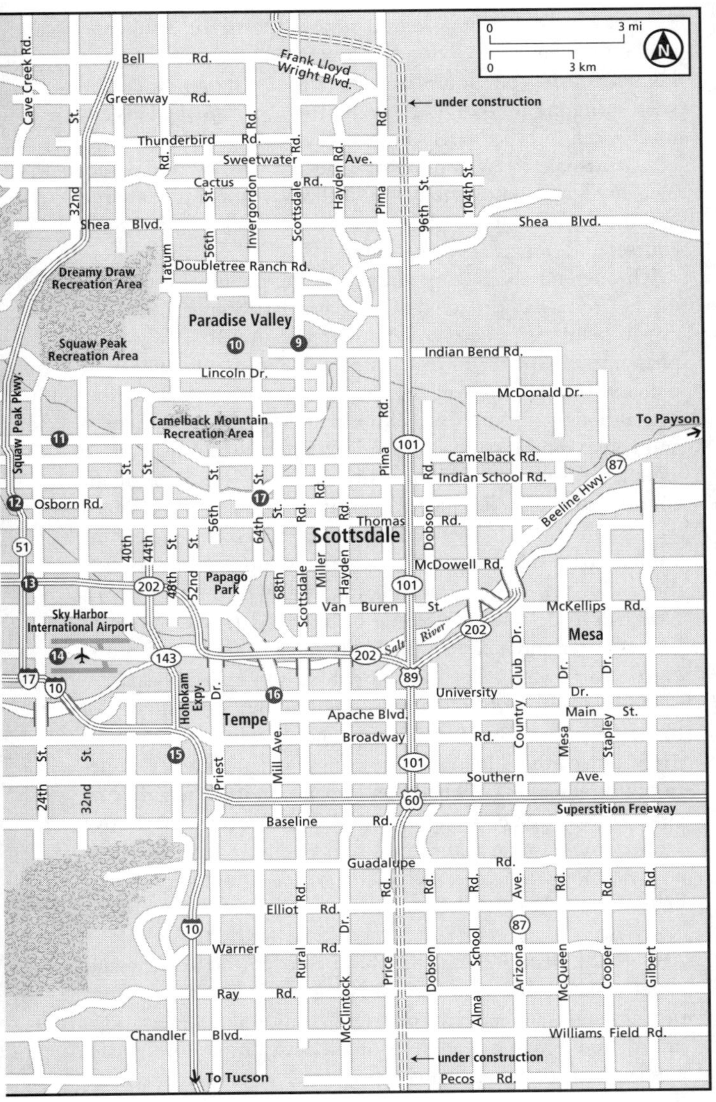

0
3 mi
0
3 km
N
under construction
Bell Rd.
Greenway Rd.
Thunderbird Rd.
Sweetwater Ave.
Cactus Rd.
Shea Blvd.
Frank Lloyd Wright Blvd.
Cave Creek Rd.
32nd St.
Tatum Blvd.
56th St.
Invergordon Rd.
Scottsdale Rd.
Hayden Rd.
Pima Rd.
96th St.
104th St.
Doubletree Ranch Rd.
Dreamy Draw Recreation Area
Paradise Valley
Squaw Peak Recreation Area
Indian Bend Rd.
Lincoln Dr.
McDonald Dr.
Camelback Mountain Recreation Area
To Payson
Squaw Peak Pkwy.
Camelback Rd.
Indian School Rd.
Osborn Rd.
Thomas Rd.
Scottsdale
Beeline Hwy.
McDowell Rd.
Papago Park
Sky Harbor International Airport
Van Buren St.
McKellips Rd.
Salt River
Mesa
Hohokam Expy.
University Dr.
Tempe
Apache Blvd.
Main St.
Broadway Rd.
Southern Ave.
Superstition Freeway
Baseline Rd.
Guadalupe Rd.
Elliot Rd.
Warner Rd.
Ray Rd.
Chandler Blvd.
Williams Field Rd.
To Tucson
Pecos Rd.
Priest Dr.
Mill Ave.
Country Club Dr.
Mesa Dr.
Stapley Dr.
Rural Rd.
McClintock Dr.
Price Rd.
Dobson Rd.
Alma School Rd.
Arizona Ave.
McQueen Rd.
Cooper Rd.
Gilbert Rd.
24th St.
40th St.
44th St.
48th St.
52nd St.
64th St.
68th St.
Miller Rd.

In Scottsdale, luxury resorts sprawl across the landscape, convertibles and SUVs clog the streets, and new golf courses, luxury housing developments, and upscale shopping centers keep springing up like wildflowers after a rainstorm. This city until recently billed itself as the West's most Western town, but Scottsdale today is more of a Beverly Hills of the desert. The city has also now sprawled all the way north to Carefree, and it is here, in north Scottsdale, that the valley's newest golf courses and resorts are to be found.

Throughout the metropolitan area, the population is growing at such a rapid pace that an alarm has been raised: Slow down before we become another Los Angeles! Why the phenomenal growth? In large part it's due to the climate. More than 300 days of sunshine a year is a powerful attraction, and although summers are blisteringly hot, the mountains—and cooler temperatures—are only 2 hours away. However, in winter the Valley of the Sun truly shines. While most of the country is frozen solid, the valley is sunny and warm. This great winter climate has helped make this area the resort capital of the United States. However, with stiff competition from resorts in the Caribbean, Mexico, and Hawaii, Valley of the Sun resorts have had to do a lot of keeping up with the Joneses in recent years. Bigger and splashier pools have been added, and nearly every resort in the valley has added a full-service health spa.

Golf, tennis, and lounging by the pool are only the tip of the iceberg (so to speak) when it comes to winter activities in the Valley of the Sun. With the cooler winter weather comes the cultural season, and between Phoenix and the neighboring cities of Scottsdale, Tempe, and Mesa, there's an impressive array of music, dance, and theater to be enjoyed. Scottsdale is also well known as a center of the visual arts, ranking only behind New York and Santa Fe in its concentration of art galleries.

Over the years, Phoenix has both enjoyed the benefits and suffered the problems of rapid urban growth. It has gone from tiny agricultural village to sprawling cosmopolitan metropolis in little more than a century. Along the way, it has lost its past amid urban sprawl and unchecked development; at the same time, it has forged a city that's quintessentially 20th-century American. Shopping malls, the gathering places of America, are raised to an art form in Phoenix. Luxurious resorts create fantasy worlds of waterfalls and swimming pools. Perhaps it's this willingness to create a new world on top of an old one that attracts people to Phoenix. Then again, maybe it's just all that sunshine.

1 Visitor Information

If you have more questions than we can answer in this book, there are a number of places that may have the answers for you. The **Visitor Information Line** (☎ **602/252-5588**) has recorded information about current events in Phoenix. However, the city's main visitor information center is the **Greater Phoenix Convention and Visitors Bureau** (☎ **877/225-5749** or 602/254-6500; www.phoenixcvb.com).

You can do additional research online by visiting the following Web sites: **CitySearch Phoenix** (www.phoenix.citysearch.com), which provides a visitors' guide of city essentials; the **Phoenix Area Guide** (http://phoenix.areaguides.net), which offers Yellow Pages, White Pages, maps, and a travel guide section; and **Phoenix Downtown** (www.downtownphx.org), which offers contact information for many downtown businesses. If you're traveling to Phoenix for business, the accommodation information and meeting planner at the **Greater Phoenix Convention & Visitors Bureau** site (www.phoenixcvb.com) might be especially helpful to you.

For statewide travel information, contact the **Arizona Office of Tourism** (☎ **800/842-8257** or 602/230-7733). The Arizona Office of Tourism's Web site is **www.arizonaguide.com**.

For visitor center and information desk locations once you arrive, see "Orientation" in chapter 3.

2 When to Go

In Phoenix and other parts of the desert, the high season runs from October to mid-May, with the highest hotel rates in effect during January and February. The spring and autumn are the all-around best times to visit because temperatures are warm without extremes. If for some reason you happen to be visiting the desert in July or August, be prepared for sudden thunderstorms. These storms often cause flash floods that make many roads briefly impassable. Road signs warning motorists not to enter low areas when flooded are meant to be taken very seriously.

Be mindful of the fact that the desert can be cold as well as hot. Although winter is the prime tourist season in Phoenix, night temperatures can be below freezing and days can even be too cold for sunning or swimming.

Phoenix's Average Temperatures (°F) & Days of Rain

	Jan	Feb	Mar	Apr	May	June	July	Aug	Sept	Oct	Nov	Dec
Avg. High	65	69	75	84	93	102	105	102	98	88	75	66
Avg. Low	38	41	45	52	60	68	78	76	69	57	45	39
Days of Rain	4	4	3	2	1	1	4	5	3	3	2	4

PHOENIX CALENDAR OF EVENTS

January

- **Phoenix Open Golf Tournament,** Scottsdale. Prestigious PGA golf tournament at the Tournament Players Club. Call ☎ **602/870-0163** for details. Mid- to late January.

February

- **Parada del Sol Parade and Rodeo,** Scottsdale. The state's longest horse-drawn parade, plus a street dance and rodeo. For more information, call ☎ **480/502-1880.** Early February.
- **World Championship Hoop Dance,** Phoenix. Native American dancers from around the nation take part in this colorful competition held at the Heard Museum. Call ☎ **602/252-8840** for details. Early February.
- **Arizona Renaissance Festival,** Apache Junction. This 16th-century English country fair has costumed participants and includes tournament jousting. Phone ☎ **520/463-2700** for details. Weekends from early February to March.
- **All-Arabian Horse Show,** Scottsdale's Westworld. A celebration of the Arabian horse. For additional information, call ☎ **480/ 515-1500** or 480/312-6802. Mid- to late February.

March

- **Heard Museum Guild Indian Fair,** Phoenix. Indian cultural and dance presentations and one of the greatest selections of Native American crafts in the Southwest make this a fascinating festival. Plus, with the festival entrance fee you get admission to the Heard Museum. Go early to avoid the crowds. Call ☎ **602/252-8840** for details. First weekend in March.

- **Franklin Templeton Tennis Classic,** Scottsdale. Top names in men's professional tennis, such as Andre Agassi and Pete Sampras, compete in this tournament at the Fairmont Scottsdale Princess hotel. For information, call ☎ **480/922-0222.** Early March.
- **Wiener Dog Nationals,** Phoenix. How 'bout those dachshunds? Watch this great low-ridin' action at the Phoenix Greyhound Park. You'll see the greyhounds run, too. Call ☎ **602/ 273-7181.** Early March.
- **Scottsdale Arts Festival,** Scottsdale Mall. This visual and performing arts festival has free concerts, an art show, and children's events. For more information, phone ☎ **480/ 994-ARTS.** Second weekend in March.
- **Welcome Back Buzzards,** Superior. A flock of turkey buzzards arrives annually at the Boyce Thompson Arboretum to roost in the eucalyptus trees, and this festival celebrates their arrival. For details, call ☎ **520/689-2723.** Late March.
- **The Tradition,** Scottsdale. This Senior PGA tournament at Cochise Course at Desert Mountain hosts the big names. Call ☎ **480/595-4070** for more information. Late March to early April.

April

- **Maricopa County Fair,** Phoenix. The Arizona State Fairgrounds hosts a midway, agricultural and livestock exhibits, and entertainment. For details, phone ☎ **602/252-0717.** Late April to early May.

May

- **Cinco de Mayo,** Phoenix. Celebration of the Mexican victory over the French in a famous 1862 battle, complete with food, music, and dancing. Call ☎ **602/262-5025** for details on the festivities in Phoenix; call ☎ **520/292-9326** for more information on the celebration in Tucson's Kennedy Park. Around May 5.

June

- **Juneteenth Festival,** Phoenix. Festival in East Lake Park celebrating African American Independence Day, including entertainment, food, and an art show. Call ☎ **602/256-3113.** Third weekend in June.

July

- **Independence Day.** For information about fireworks displays in Phoenix, call ☎ **602/534-FEST.** July 4.

August

- **5th Annual Navajo Nation Day,** Chris-Town Mall, Phoenix. Silversmiths, potters, and kachina carvers display and sell art. For details, call ☎ **602/242-9074**. First weekend in August.

September

- **Scottsdale Center for the Arts Annual Gala.** Jazz, ballet, music, art exhibits, and special events. Phone ☎ **480/994-2787** for further information. Late September.

October

- **Coors Rodeo Showdown,** Phoenix. Top rodeo stars compete in this world finals rodeo at the America West Arena. For details, call ☎ **800/946-9711.** Mid- to late October.
- **Arizona State Fair,** Phoenix. This shindig at the Arizona State Fairgrounds features rodeos, top-name entertainment, and ethnic food. Phone ☎ **602/252-6771** for more information. Late October to early November.
- **Annual Cowboy Artists of America Exhibition,** Phoenix. The Phoenix Art Museum hosts the most prestigious and best-known Western art show in the region. For details, call ☎ **602/257-1222.** Late October.

November

- **Thunderbird Balloon Classic,** Scottsdale. More than 150 hot-air balloons fill the Arizona sky. Call ☎ **602/978-7330** or 602/978-7208 for details. Early November.

December

- **Fiesta Bowl Parade,** Phoenix. Huge, nationally televised parade, featuring floats and marching bands. Phone ☎ **800/635-5748** or 480/350-0900 for more information. December 31.

3 Tips for Travelers with Special Needs

FOR TRAVELERS WITH DISABILITIES When making airline reservations, always mention your disability. Airline policies differ regarding wheelchairs and guide dogs. Most hotels now offer wheelchair-accessible accommodations, and some of the larger and more expensive resorts also offer TDD telephones and other amenities for the hearing and sight impaired.

A World of Options, a book of resources for travelers with disabilities, covers everything from biking trips to scuba outfitters. It costs $35 ($30 for members) and is available

Staying Healthy

If you've never been to the desert before, you should be sure to prepare yourself for this harsh environment. No matter what time of year it is, the desert sun is strong and bright. Use sunscreen when you're outdoors—particularly if you're up in the mountains, where the altitude makes sunburn more likely. The bright sun also makes sunglasses a necessity.

Even if you don't feel hot in the desert, the dry air steals moisture from your body, so drink plenty of fluids. You may want to use a body lotion as well. Skin dries out quickly in the desert air.

---

from **Mobility International USA,** P.O. Box 10767, Eugene, OR, 97440 (☎ **541/343-1284,** voice and TDD; www. miusa. org). Annual membership for Mobility International is $35, which includes its biannual newsletter, *Over the Rainbow.*

Travelin' Talk Network, P.O. Box 1796, Wheat Ridge, CO 80034 (☎ **303/232-2979;** www.travelintalk.net), operates a Web site for travelers with disabilities, and each month, e-mails a newsletter ($19.95 per year) with information about discounts, accessible hotels, trip companions, and other traveling tips. Those without Internet access can also subscribe and receive the newsletter by mail every other month. Another online newsletter and database, **www.access-able.com**, is operated by the same company and supplies information about trip planning, accessible cruise ships, and travel agents that specialize in trips for people with disabilities.

Many of the major car-rental companies now offer hand-controlled cars for drivers with disabilities. Avis can provide such a vehicle at any of its locations in the United States with 48-hour advance notice; Hertz requires between 24 and 72 hours of advance reservation at most of its locations. **Wheelchair Getaways** (☎ **800/642-2042;** www.wheelchair-getaways. com) rents specialized vans with wheelchair lifts and other features for travelers with disabilities in about 38 cities across the United States.

Travelers with disabilities might also want to consider joining a tour that caters specifically to them. **Accessible Journeys** (☎ **800/TINGLES** or 610/521-0339), for slow walkers and wheelchair travelers, offers excursions to the Phoenix area.

FOR GAY MEN & LESBIANS To get in touch with Phoenix's gay and lesbian community, you can contact the **Gay and Lesbian Community Center,** 24 W. Camelback Rd., Suite C (☎ **602/265-7283**). At the community center and at gay bars around Phoenix, you can pick up various community publications, including *Echo* and *Heat Stroke.*

FOR SENIORS When making airline reservations, always mention that you're a senior citizen—many airlines offer discounts. You should also carry some sort of photo ID card (driver's license, passport, and so on) to avail yourself of senior-citizen discounts on attractions, hotels, motels, and public transportation.

If you aren't a member of the **American Association of Retired Persons (AARP),** 601 E St. NW, Washington, DC 20049 (☎ **800/424-3410** or 202/424-3410), you should consider joining. This association provides discounts for many lodgings, car rentals, airfares, and attractions, although you can sometimes get a similar discount simply by showing your ID.

The Mature Traveler, a monthly 12-page newsletter on senior citizen travel, is a valuable resource. It is available by subscription ($32 a year) from GEM Publishing Group, Box 50400, Reno, NV 89513-0400. GEM also publishes ***The Book of Deals,*** a collection of more than 1,000 senior discounts on airlines, lodging, tours, and attractions around the country; it's available for $9.90 by calling ☎ **800/460-6676.**

Grand Circle Travel is another of the literally hundreds of travel agencies specializing in vacations for seniors (347 Congress St., Boston, MA 02210 (☎ **800/221-2610** or 617/350-7500). *But beware:* Many of them are of the tour-bus variety, with free trips thrown in for those who organize groups of 20 or more. Seniors seeking more independent travel should probably consult a regular travel agent. **SAGA International Holidays,** 222 Berkeley St., Boston, MA 02116 (☎ **800/343-0273**), offers inclusive tours and cruises for those 50 and older. SAGA also sponsors the more substantial "Road Scholar Tours," which are fun loving but with an educational bent, and is an agent for Smithsonian Institution tours.

If you'd like to do a bit of studying on vacation in the company of like-minded older travelers, consider looking into **Elderhostel,** 75 Federal St., Boston, MA 02110 (☎ **877/426-8056;** www.elderhostel.org).

4 Getting There

BY PLANE

THE MAJOR AIRLINES Phoenix is served by most major airlines, including **Aero México** (☎ 800/237-6639), **Alaska Airlines** (☎ 800/426-0333), **America West** (☎ 800/235-9292), **American** (☎ 800/433-7300), **Continental** (☎ 800/525-0280), **Delta** (☎ 800/221-1212), **Frontier Airlines** (☎ 800/432-1359), **Northwest/KLM** (☎ 800/225-2525), **Shuttle by United** (☎ 800/748-8853, **Southwest** (☎ 800/435-9792), **TWA** (☎ 800/221-2000), **United** (☎ 800/241-6522), and **US Airways** (☎ 800/428-4322).

FINDING THE BEST AIRFARES There are a few easy ways to save on the cost of airfare. You can start by checking your newspaper for advertised discounts or call the airlines directly and ask if any promotional rates or special fares are available. If your schedule is flexible, ask if you can secure a chaper fare by staying an extra day or by flying midweek. (Many airlines won't volunteer this information.) Note, however, that the lowest-priced fares often are non-refundable, require advance purchase of 1 to 3 weeks and a certain length of stay, and carry penalties for changing dates of travel.

Consolidators, also known as bucket shops, are a good place to find low fares. Consolidators buy seats in bulk from the airlines and then sell them back to the public at prices below even the airlines' discounted rates. Their small boxed ads usually run in the Sunday travel section of newspapers at the bottom of the page. Before you pay, however, ask for a confirmation number from the consolidator and then call the airline itself to confirm your seat. Be prepared to book your ticket with a different consolidator—there are many to choose from—if the airline can't confirm your reservation. Also be aware that bucket shop tickets are usually nonrefundable or rigged with stiff cancellation penalties, often as high as 50% to 75% of the ticket price. And when an airline runs a special deal, you won't always do better with a consolidator.

For discount and last-minute bookings, contact **McCord Consumer Direct** (☎ **800/FLY-ASAP** or 800/454-7700; www.better1.com), which can often get you tickets at significantly less than full fare. **1-800-airfare** (www.1800airfare.com) was formerly owned by TWA but now offers the deepest discounts on many other airlines and can sometimes provide

Money-Saving Tips

Planning a winter vacation in Phoenix can easily induce sticker shock. However, there are a few sun-country options for vacationers on a tight budget.

- If you don't absolutely have to have all the amenities of a big resort, there are endless chain motel options in the Phoenix area. However, even these accommodations are often overpriced for what you get. Still, you'll be in the sun, and you'll likely have a pool for cooling off.
- You can save a substantial amount on hotel rates by joining the American Automobile Association (AAA). The savings on just a few nights' lodging can cover the cost of the annual AAA membership.
- To avoid ATM fees, use your card as a debit card at a grocery store and get cash back from your purchase.
- Have lunch at an expensive restaurant, and you'll be able savor the ambience at a fraction of the cost of dinner. Often the lunch menu includes some items from the dinner menu at much lower prices.
- Ask when hotel room rates drop for the summer and schedule your trip for right after the rates go down (or just before they go back up in the fall). Many resorts also have a short discounted season just before Christmas. Travel then and you can save hundreds of dollars over a visit in January.
- Pick up rental cars somewhere other than the Phoenix airports. Rental car companies operating inside the airport charge 20% or more in taxes and service fees. Taxes and service charges outside the airport are about half as much.

a next-day ticket. There are also "rebators," such as **Travel Avenue** (☎ **800/333-3335** or 312/876-1116), which rebate part of their commissions to you.

Another way to find cheap fares is to search the Internet. **Travelocity** (www.travelocity.com or www.frommers.travelocity.com), Frommer's online travel planning and booking partner, uses the SABRE computer reservations system that most travel agents use, and it has a "Last Minute Deals" database that advertises really cheap fares for those who can get away at a moment's notice. **Expedia** (expedia.com), Travelocity's major competitor, offers several ways of obtaining the best possible fares, including a Fare Calendar, which helps you plan your trip around the best possible fares. Other helpful sites include **TRIP.com** (www.trip.com) and **Yahoo! Travel** (www.travel.yahoo.com).

Last-minute deals are also available through free e-mail services, provided directly by the airlines. Each week, the airline sends you a list of discounted flights, usually leaving the upcoming Friday or Saturday and returning the following Monday or Tuesday. You can sign up for all the major airlines at once by logging on to **Smarter Living** (www.smarterliving.com) or **1travel.com** (www.1travel.com), or visit each individual airline's Web site.

SKY HARBOR AIRPORT Centrally located 3 miles from downtown Phoenix, Sky Harbor Airport has three terminals, and in these three terminals you'll find car-rental desks, information desks, hotel-reservation centers with direct lines to various valley hotels, and a food court. There's a free 24-hour shuttle bus operating every 5 to 10 minutes between the three terminals (less frequently during the night). For general airport information, call ☎ **602/273-3300;** for airport paging, call **602/273-3456;** for lost and found, call **602/273-3307.**

There are two entrances to the airport. The west entrance can be accessed from either the Squaw Peak Parkway (Ariz. 51) or 24th Street, and the east entrance can be accessed from the Hohokam Expressway (Ariz. 143), which is an extension of 44th Street. If you're headed to downtown Phoenix, leave by way of the 24th Street exit and continue west on Washington Street. If you're headed to Scottsdale, take the 24th Street exit, go north on the Squaw Peak Parkway to the Indian School Road or Lincoln Drive exit, and then drive east, or get on the 202 east loop to 101 north. For Tempe or Mesa, take the 44th Street exit.

If you want to come and go in style, you can arrange to have a stretch limo pick you up and take you back to the airport (or anywhere else in town, for that matter). **Transtyle** (☎ **800/410-5479** or 480/948-6131) charges a flat fee of $120 between the airport and most Phoenix and Scottsdale resorts.

SuperShuttle (☎ **800/BLUE-VAN** or 602/244-9000) offers 24-hour door-to-door van service between Sky Harbor Airport and resorts, hotels, and homes throughout the valley.

Fares average about $7 to $10 to the downtown and Tempe area (about $6 for each additional person), and about $14 to $28 per person to Scottsdale and the northern area of the city. When heading back to the airport for a departure, call in advance (☎ **602/244-9000**).

Taxis can also be found waiting outside all three airport terminals, or you can call **Yellow Cab** (☎ **602/252-5252**) or **Checker Cab** (☎ **602/257-1818**).

Valley Metro provides **public bus service** throughout the valley with the Red Line (R) operating between the airport and downtown Phoenix, Tempe, and Mesa. The Red Line operates daily between about 5am and 10pm. You can pick up a copy of *The Bus Book,* a guide and route map for the Valley Metro bus system, at Central Station, at the corner of Central Avenue and Van Buren Street.

BY CAR

Phoenix is connected to Los Angeles and Tucson by I-10 and to Flagstaff via I-17. If you're headed to Scottsdale, the easiest route is to take the Red Mountain Freeway (Ariz. 202) east to U.S. 101 north. U.S. 101 will eventually loop all the way around the north side of the valley. The Superstition Freeway (U.S. 60) leads to Tempe, Mesa, and Chandler.

The distance to Phoenix from Los Angeles is approximately 369 miles; from San Francisco, 778 miles; from Albuquerque, 455 miles; from Salt Lake City, 660 miles; from Las Vegas, 287 miles; and from Santa Fe, 516 miles.

If you're planning to drive through northern Arizona anytime in the winter, bring tire chains.

BY TRAIN

Phoenix has **Amtrak** (☎ **800/872-7245** in the United States and Canada for information and reservations; www.amtrak.com) service from Los Angeles to the west and Albuquerque, Santa Fe, Kansas City, and Chicago to the east aboard the Southwest Chief. The Sunset Limited connects Orlando, New Orleans, Houston, San Antonio, El Paso, and Los Angeles with Phoenix. The train stops in Flagstaff or Tucson, and passengers must take a shuttle bus to Phoenix. Amtrak connector buses arrive and depart from the old Phoenix **Amtrak railroad terminal,** 401 W. Harrison St. (☎ **800/872-7245** or 602/253-0121; www.amtrak.com).

At press time, the fare from Los Angeles to Phoenix was between $37 and $104 one-way and $74 to $208 round-trip. This trip, including shuttle bus, can take between 12 and 19 hours, depending on the schedule. Earlier bookings secure lower fares.

5 For Foreign Visitors

ENTRY REQUIREMENTS

Immigration law is a hot political issue in the United States these days, and the following requirements may have changed somewhat by the time you plan your trip. Check at any U.S. embassy or consulate for current information and requirements. You can also plug into the **U.S. State Department's** Internet site at **www.state.gov**.

VISAS The U.S. State Department has a **Visa Waiver Pilot Program** allowing citizens of certain countries to enter the United States without a visa for stays of up to 90 days. At press time, these countries included Andorra, Argentina, Australia, Austria, Belgium, Brunei, Denmark, Finland, France, Germany, Iceland, Ireland, Italy, Japan, Liechtenstein, Luxembourg, Monaco, the Netherlands, New Zealand, Norway, San Marino, Slovenia, Spain, Sweden, Switzerland, and the United Kingdom. Citizens of these countries need only a valid passport and a round-trip air or cruise ticket in their possession upon arrival. If they first enter the United States, they may also visit Mexico, Canada, Bermuda, and/or the Caribbean islands and return to the United States without a visa. Further information is available from any U.S. embassy or consulate. Canadian citizens may enter the United States without visas; they need only proof of residence.

Citizens of all other countries must have (1) a valid passport that expires at least 6 months later than the scheduled end of their visit to the United States, and (2) a tourist visa, which can be obtained without charge from any U.S. consulate.

OBTAINING A VISA To get a visa, the traveler must submit a completed application form (either in person or by mail) with a 1½-inch-square photo, and must demonstrate binding ties to a residence abroad. Usually you can get a visa at once or within 24 hours, but it may take longer during the summer rush from June through August. If you cannot go in person, contact the nearest U.S. embassy or consulate for directions on applying by mail. Your travel agent or airline office may also be able to supply you with visa applications and instructions. The U.S. consulate or embassy that issues your visa determines whether you will be issued a multiple- or single-entry visa and any restrictions on the length of your stay.

British subjects can get up-to-date passport and visa information by calling the **U.S. Embassy Visa Information Line** (☎ **0891/200-290**) or the **London Passport Office** (☎ **020/7271-3000** for recorded information).

MEDICAL REQUIREMENTS Unless you're arriving from an area known to be suffering from an epidemic (particularly cholera or yellow fever), inoculations or vaccinations are not required for entry into the United States. If you have a disease that requires treatment with narcotics or syringe-administered medications, carry a valid signed prescription from your physician to allay any suspicions that you may be smuggling narcotics (a serious offense that carries severe penalties in the United States).

DRIVER'S LICENSES Foreign driver's licenses are mostly recognized in the United States, although you may want to get an international driver's license if your home license is not written in English.

CUSTOMS REQUIREMENTS Every visitor over 21 years of age may bring in, free of duty, the following: (1) 1 liter of wine or hard liquor; (2) 200 cigarettes, 100 cigars (but not from Cuba), or 3 pounds of smoking tobacco; and (3) $100 worth of gifts. These exemptions are offered to travelers who spend at least 72 hours in the United States and who have not claimed them within the preceding 6 months. It is altogether forbidden to bring into the country foodstuffs (particularly fruit, cooked meats, and canned goods) and plants (vegetables, seeds, tropical plants, and the like). Foreign tourists may bring in or take out up to $10,000 in U.S. or foreign currency with no formalities; larger sums must be declared to U.S. Customs on entering or leaving, which includes filing form CM 4790. For more specific information regarding U.S. Customs, call your nearest U.S. embassy or consulate, or contact the **U.S. Customs** office at ☎ **202/927-1770** or **www.customs.gov/travel/travel.htm**.

INSURANCE

Although it's not required of travelers, health insurance is highly recommended. Unlike many European countries, the United States does not usually offer free or low-cost medical care to its citizens or visitors. Doctors and hospitals are expensive, and in most cases require advance payment or proof of coverage before they render their services. Other policies can cover everything from the loss or theft of your baggage and trip cancellation to the guarantee of bail in case you're arrested. Good policies also cover the costs of an accident, repatriation, or death. Packages such as **Europ Assistance** in Europe are sold by automobile clubs and travel agencies at attractive rates. **Worldwide Assistance Services** (☎ **800/821-2828**) is the agent for Europ Assistance in the United States.

Although lack of health insurance may prevent you from being admitted to a hospital in non-emergencies, don't worry about being left on a street corner to die: The American way is to fix you now and bill the living daylights out of you later.

MONEY

CURRENCY The U.S. monetary system has a decimal base: one American **dollar** ($1) = 100 **cents** (100¢).

Dollar bills commonly come in $1 (a "buck"), $5, $10, $20, $50, and $100 denominations (the last two are not welcome when paying for small purchases and are not accepted in taxis). There are also $2 bills (seldom encountered).

There are six denominations of coins: 1¢ (1 cent, or a "penny"), 5¢ (5 cents, or a "nickel"), 10¢ (10 cents, or a "dime"), 25¢ (25 cents, or a "quarter"), 50¢ (50 cents, or a "half dollar"), and $1 coins, of which there are three types in circulation (the older, large Eisenhower dollar, the smaller Susan B. Anthony dollar, and the new golden Sacagawea dollar). Note that U.S. coins are not stamped with their numeric value.

The foreign-exchange bureaus so common in Europe are rare even at airports in the United States, and nonexistent outside major cities. Try to avoid having to change foreign money or traveler's checks not denominated in U.S. dollars at a small-town bank or even a branch bank in a big city. In fact, leave any currency other than U.S. dollars at home—it could prove more nuisance to you than it's worth.

TRAVELER'S CHECKS Traveler's checks *denominated in U.S. dollars* are readily accepted at most hotels, motels, restaurants, and large stores, but might not be accepted at small stores or for small purchases. The best place to change traveler's checks is at a bank. Do not bring traveler's checks denominated in other currencies. The three traveler's checks that are most widely recognized are **Visa, American Express,** and **Thomas Cook.**

CREDIT CARDS Credit cards are the most widely used form of payment in the United States: **Visa** (BarclayCard in Britain), **MasterCard** (Eurocard in Europe, Access in Britain, Chargex in Canada), **American Express, Diners Club, Discover,** and **Carte Blanche.** You must have a credit or charge card to rent a car. There are, however, a handful of stores and restaurants that do not take credit cards, so be sure to ask in advance. Most businesses display a sticker near their entrance to let you know which cards they accept. (*Note:* Often businesses require a minimum purchase price, usually around $10, to use a credit card.)

It is strongly recommended that you bring at least one major credit card. Hotels, car-rental companies, and airlines usually require a credit-card imprint as a deposit against expenses, and in an emergency a credit card can be priceless.

GETTING TO THE UNITED STATES

Airlines with direct or connecting service from London to Phoenix (along with their phone numbers in Great Britain) include **American** (☎ 0345/567-567; www.americanair.com), **British Airways** (☎ 0345/222-111; www.britishairways.com), **Continental** (☎ 0800/776-464; www.flycontinental.com), **Delta** (☎ 0800/414-767; www.delta.com), **TWA** (☎ 020/8814-0707 in London, or 0800/221-2000; www.twa.com), **United** (☎ 020/8990-9900 in London, or 0800/888-555 outside London; www.ual.com), and **US Airways** (☎ 0800/783-5556; www.usairways.com).

From Canada there are flights to Phoenix from Toronto on **Air Canada** (☎ 888/247-2262; www.aircanada.ca), **American** (☎ 800/433-7300; www.americanair.com), **Delta** (☎ 800/221-1212; www.delta.com), **Northwest** (☎ 800/225-2525; www.nwa.com), **TWA** (☎ 800/221-2000; www.twa.com), **United** (☎ 800/241-6522; www.ual.com), and **US Airways** (☎ 800/428-4322; usairways.com), and from Vancouver on **Alaska Airlines** (☎ 800/426-0333; www.alaskaair.com), **America West** (☎ 800/235-9292; www.americawest.com), **Canadian Airlines** (☎ 800/426-7000; www.cdnair.ca), **Northwest,** and **United.**

From New Zealand and Australia, there are flights to Los Angeles on **Qantas** (☎ 13 13 13; www.qantas.com.au) and **Air New Zealand** (☎ 0800/737-000 in Auckland; www.airnewzealand.co.nz). Continue on to Phoenix on a regional airline such as **America West** (☎ 800/235-9292; www.americawest.com) or **Southwest** (☎ 800/435-9792; www.southwest.com).

AIRLINE DISCOUNTS Travelers from overseas can take advantage of the **advance-purchase excursion (APEX)** fares offered by the major U.S. and European carriers. For more money-saving airline advice, see "Getting There," earlier in this chapter.

IMMIGRATION & CUSTOMS CLEARANCE The visitor arriving by air, no matter what the port of entry, should cultivate patience before setting foot on U.S. soil. Getting through Immigration Control might take as long as 2 hours on some days, especially summer weekends. Add the time it takes to clear Customs, and you'll see that you should make a very generous allowance for delay in planning connections between international and domestic flights—an average of 2 to 3 hours at least.

In contrast, travelers arriving by car or by rail from Canada will find border-crossing formalities streamlined practically to the vanishing point. And air travelers from Canada, Bermuda, and some places in the Caribbean can sometimes go through Customs and Immigration at the point of departure, which is much quicker.

GETTING AROUND THE UNITED STATES

For specific information on traveling to and around Phoenix, see "Getting There" and "Getting Around," earlier in this chapter.

BY PLANE Some large airlines (for example, United and Delta) offer travelers on their transatlantic or transpacific flights special discount tickets under the name **Visit USA,** allowing mostly one-way travel from one U.S. destination to another at very low prices. These discount tickets are not on sale in the United States and must be purchased abroad in conjunction with your international ticket. This system is the best, easiest, and fastest way to see the United States at low cost. You should get information well in advance from your travel agent or the office of the airline concerned, since the conditions attached to these discount tickets can be changed without advance notice.

BY CAR The United States is a car culture through and through. Driving is the most cost-effective, convenient, and comfortable way to travel through the West. The interstate highway system connects cities and towns all over the country, and in addition to these high-speed, limited-access roadways, there's an extensive network of federal, state, and local highways and roads. Driving will give you a lot of flexibility in making, and altering, your itinerary and in allowing you to see some off-the-beaten-path destinations that cannot be reached easily by public transportation. You'll also have easy access to inexpensive motels at interstate highway off-ramps.

BY TRAIN International visitors can also buy a **USA Railpass,** good for 15 or 30 days of unlimited travel on **Amtrak** (☎ **800/USA-RAIL**). The pass is available through many foreign travel agents. Prices in 2000 for a 15-day pass are $295 off-peak, $440 peak; a 30-day pass costs $385 off-peak, $550 peak. (With a foreign passport, you can also buy passes at some Amtrak offices in the United States, including locations in San Francisco, Los Angeles, Chicago, New York, Miami, Boston, and Washington, D.C.) Reservations are generally required and should be made for each part of your trip as early as possible. Amtrak also offers an **Air/Rail Travel Plan** that allows you to travel by both train and plane; for information call ☎ **800/440-8202.**

BY BUS Although bus travel is often the most economical form of public transit for short hops between U.S. cities, it can also be slow and uncomfortable—certainly not an option for everyone (particularly when Amtrak, which is far more luxurious, offers similar rates). **Greyhound/Trailways** (☎ **800/231-2222**), the sole nationwide bus line, offers an **Ameripass** for unlimited travel for 7 days at $169, 15 days at $249, 30 days at $349, and 60 days at $479. Passes must be purchased at a Greyhound terminal. Special rates are available for senior citizens and students.

3

Getting to Know Phoenix & Scottsdale

This chapter provides an overview of the Phoenix metropolitan area, with plenty of advice on how to navigate your way through its sprawl, and the best places to stay and dine in the Valley of the Sun. You'll also find a list of useful resources, from weather information to hospital and pharmacy locations.

1 Orientation

VISITOR INFORMATION

You'll find **tourist information desks** in the baggage claim areas of all three terminals at Sky Harbor Airport. The city's main visitor information center, the **Greater Phoenix Convention and Visitors Bureau,** is located at 50 N. Second St., on the corner of Adams Street in downtown Phoenix (☎ **602/254-6500**). The city also operates a small visitor center at the Biltmore Fashion Park shopping center at the corner of Camelback Road and 24th Street (☎ **602/955-1963**).

If you're staying in Scottsdale, you may want to contact or drop by the **Scottsdale Chamber of Commerce and Visitors Center,** 7343 Scottsdale Mall, Scottsdale, AZ 85251-4498 (☎ **800/877-1117** or 480/945-8481; www.scottsdalecvb.com).

CITY LAYOUT

MAIN ARTERIES & STREETS Over the past decade, the Phoenix area has seen the construction of numerous new freeways. It is now possible to drive from the airport to Scottsdale by freeway rather than having to deal with stoplights and local traffic. U.S. 101, which currently exists only in two unconnected sections (one between Tempe and Scottsdale and the other between north Phoenix and Peoria on the east side of the valley) will eventually form a loop around the east, north, and west sides of the valley, providing freeway access to Scottsdale from I-17 on the north side of Phoenix and from U.S. 60 in Tempe.

I-17 (Black Canyon Freeway), which connects Phoenix with Flagstaff, is the city's main north-south freeway. This freeway curves to the east just south of downtown (where it is renamed the **Maricopa Freeway** and merges with I-10). **I-10,** which connects Phoenix with Los Angeles and Tucson, is called the **Papago Freeway** on the west side of the valley and as it passes north of downtown; as it curves around to pass south of the airport, it merges with I-17 and is renamed the Maricopa Freeway. At Tempe, this freeway curves around to the south and heads out of the valley.

North of the airport, **Arizona 202 (Red Mountain Freeway)** heads east from I-10 and passes along the north side of Tempe, providing access to downtown Tempe, Arizona State University, Mesa, and Scottsdale (via U.S. 101). On the east side of the airport, **Arizona 143 (Hohokam Expressway)** connects Arizona 202 with I-10.

At the interchange of I-10 and Arizona 202, northwest of Sky Harbor Airport, **Arizona 51 (Squaw Peak Freeway)** heads north through the center of Phoenix and is the best north-south route in the city. This freeway is currently being extended north from Bell Road and will eventually link up with the U.S. 101 loop.

Just south of the airport, **U.S. 60 (Superstition Freeway)** heads east to Tempe, Chandler, Mesa, and Gilbert. **U.S. 101** leads north from U.S. 60 (and Ariz. 202) toward Scottsdale.

Impressions

As the mythical phoenix rose reborn from its ashes, so shall a great civilization rise here on the ashes of a past civilization. I name thee Phoenix.

—"Lord" Bryan Philip Darrel Duppa,
the British settler who named Phoenix

This freeway is currently being extended north from Shea Boulevard and now provides the best route from the airport to the Scottsdale resorts.

Secondary highways in the valley include the **Beeline Highway (Ariz. 87),** which starts out as Country Club Drive in Mesa and leads to Payson, and **Grand Avenue (U.S. 60),** which starts downtown and leads to Sun City and Wickenburg.

Phoenix and the surrounding cities of Mesa, Tempe, Scottsdale, and Chandler, and even those cities farther out in the valley, are laid out in a grid pattern with major avenues and roads about every mile. For traveling east to west across Phoenix, your best choices (other than the above-mentioned freeways) are Camelback Road, Indian School Road, and McDowell Road. For traveling north and south, 44th Street, 24th Street, and Central Avenue are good choices. Hayden Road is a north-south alternative to Scottsdale Road, which gets jammed at rush hours.

FINDING AN ADDRESS **Central Avenue,** which runs north to south through downtown Phoenix, is the starting point for all east and west street numbering. **Washington Street** is the starting point for north and south numbering. North-to-south numbered *streets* are to be found on the east side of the city, while north-to-south numbered *avenues* will be found on the west. For the most part, street numbers change by 100 with each block. Odd-numbered addresses are on the south and east sides of streets, while even-numbered addresses are on north and west sides of streets.

For example, if you're looking for 4454 East Camelback Rd., you'll find it 44 blocks east of Central Avenue between 44th and 45th streets on the north side of the street. If you're looking for 2905 North 35th Ave., you'll find it 35 blocks west of Central Avenue and 29 blocks north of Washington Street on the east side of the street. Just for general reference, Camelback marks the 5000 block north.

STREET MAPS The street maps handed out by rental-car companies are almost useless for finding anything in Phoenix, so as soon as you can, stop in at a minimart and buy a Phoenix map. Unfortunately, you'll probably also have to buy a separate Scottsdale map. You can also get a simple map at either one of the airport tourist information desks or at the downtown visitor information center.

NEIGHBORHOODS IN BRIEF

Because of urban sprawl, Phoenix has yielded its importance to the Valley of the Sun, an area encompassing Phoenix and its metropolitan area of more than 20 cities. Consequently, neighborhoods, per se, have lost much of their significance as outlying cities have taken on regional importance. However, this said, there are some neighborhoods worth noting.

Downtown Phoenix Roughly bordered by Thomas Road on the north, Buckeye Road on the south, 19th Avenue on the west, and Seventh Street on the east, downtown is primarily a business, financial, and government district, where both the city hall and state capitol are located. However, in the past few years, downtown Phoenix has been rising from the ashes of neglect and positioning itself as the valley's prime sports, entertainment, and museum district. The Arizona Diamondbacks play big-league baseball in the **Bank-One Ballpark (BOB),** while the Phoenix Suns shoot hoops at the **America West Arena.** There are three major performing arts venues—the historic **Orpheum Theatre, Phoenix Symphony Hall,** and the **Herberger Theater Center.** At the Arizona Center shopping and entertainment plaza, there is a huge multiplex movie theater. Downtown museums include the **Phoenix Museum of History** and the **Arizona Science Center,** both of which are located in Heritage and Science Park. Other attractions in the downtown area include **Heritage Square** (historic homes), the **Arizona State Capitol Museum,** and **the Arizona Mining & Mineral Museum.** On the northern edge of downtown are the **Heard Museum,** the **Phoenix Central Library** (an architectural gem), and the **Phoenix Art Museum.**

Biltmore District The Biltmore District, also known as the **Camelback Corridor,** centers along Camelback Road between 24th and 44th streets and is Phoenix's upscale shopping, residential, and business district. The area is characterized by modern office buildings and is anchored by the Arizona Biltmore Hotel and Biltmore Fashion Park shopping mall.

Scottsdale A separate city of more than 200,000 people, Scottsdale extends from Tempe in the south to Carefree in the north, a distance of more than 20 miles. Scottsdale Road between Indian School Road and Shea Boulevard has long been known as **"Resort Row"** and is home to more than a dozen major resorts. However, as Scottsdale has sprawled ever northward, so, too, have resorts been opening in north Scottsdale. **Old Scottsdale** capitalizes on its cowboy heritage and has become the valley's main shopping district, with boutiques, jewelers, Native American crafts stores, souvenir shops, and numerous restaurants.

Tempe Tempe is the home of Arizona State University and has all the trappings of a university town. Nightclubs and bars abound here. The center of activity, both day and night, is **Mill Avenue,** which has dozens of interesting shops along a stretch of about 4 blocks. This is one of the few areas in the valley where locals actually walk the streets and hang out at sidewalk cafes (Old Town Scottsdale often has people on its streets, but few are locals).

Paradise Valley If Scottsdale is Phoenix's Beverly Hills, then Paradise Valley is its Bel-Air. The most exclusive neighborhood in the valley is almost entirely residential, but you won't see too many of the more lavish homes because they're set on large tracts of land.

Mesa This eastern suburb of Phoenix is the Valley's main high-tech area. Large shopping malls, many inexpensive motels, and a couple of small museums attract both locals and visitors to Mesa.

Glendale Located west of Phoenix proper, Glendale has numerous historic buildings in its downtown and has, with its dozens of antiques stores, become the antiques capital of the valley.

Carefree & Cave Creek Located about 20 miles north of Old Scottsdale, these two communities represent the Old West and the New West. Carefree is a planned community and is home to the prestigious Boulders resort and El Pedregal shopping center. Cave Creek plays up its Western heritage in its architecture and preponderance of bars, steakhouses, and shops selling Western crafts and other gifts.

2 Getting Around

BY CAR

Phoenix and the surrounding cities that together make up the Valley of the Sun sprawl over more than 400 square miles, so if you want to make the best use of your time, it's essential to have a car. Outside downtown Phoenix, there's almost always plenty of free parking wherever you go (although finding a parking space can be time consuming in Old Scottsdale and at some of the more popular malls and shopping plazas).

RENTALS All the major rental-car companies have offices in Phoenix, with desks inside the airline terminals at Sky Harbor Airport, and because this is a major tourist destination, there are often excellent rates. The best rates are those reserved at least a week in advance, but car-rental companies change rates frequently as demand goes up and down. Rates for rental cars vary considerably between companies and with the model you want to rent, the dates you rent, and your pickup and drop-off points. If you call the same company three times and ask about renting the same model car, you may get three different quotes, depending on current availability of vehicles. It pays to start shopping early and ask lots of questions—rental agents don't always volunteer information about how to save, so you have to experiment with all the parameters.

If you're a member of a frequent-flyer program, check to see which rental-car companies participate in your program. Also, when making a reservation, be sure to mention any discount you might be eligible for, such as corporate, military, or AAA, or any specials offered. Beware of coupons offering discounts on rental-car rates—they often discount the highest rates only. It's always cheaper to rent by the week, so even if you don't need a car for 7 days, you might find that it's still cheaper than renting for 4 days only.

Taxes on car rentals vary between 10% and 24% or more and are always at the high end at the Phoenix airport. You can save up to 10% (the airport concession fee recoupment charge) by renting your car at an office outside the airport. Be sure to ask about the tax and the loss-damage waiver (LDW) if you want to know what your total rental cost will be before making a reservation.

All the major rental-car companies have offices at Sky Harbor Airport as well as other locations in the Phoenix area. Among them are the following: **Alamo** (☎ 800/327-9633, 602/273-9690, or 602/244-0897); **Avis** (☎ 800/331-1212 or 602/273-3222); **Budget** (☎ 800/527-0700 or 602/267-4000); **Dollar** (☎ 800/800-4000 or 602/275-7588); **Enterprise** (☎ 800/736-8222 or 602/225-0588); **Hertz** (☎ 800/654-3131 or 602/267-8822); **National** (☎ 800/227-7368 or 602/275-4771); and **Thrifty** (☎ 800/367-2277 or 602/244-0311).

If you'd like a bit more style while you cruise from resort to golf course to nightclub to wherever, how about a Corvette? **Rent-a-Vette,** 1215 N. Scottsdale Rd., Tempe (☎ **480/941-3001**), can put you behind the wheel of a car that will get you a bit more respect from valet parking attendants at area restaurants. A Corvette will run you $149 to $249 a day. Rent-a-Vette also rents Porsche Boxters, Mustang GTs, Jaguars XKAs, and Plymouth Prowlers, with the rate at $249 a day for a Prowler.

At the rugged end of the car-rental spectrum is **Arizona Jeep & Hummer,** 7677 N. 16th St., Phoenix (☎ **602/674-8469**), which rents Jeep Wranglers for $99 to $129 for a half day or $149 to $169 for a full day and Hummers for $199 for a half day and $299 for a full day. Rates go down the more days you rent, and special lower rates are sometimes available. Along with your rental, you can get a trail book and directions for various trails into the desert. For two or more people, this is an economical alternative to doing a Jeep tour.

If a Jeep still doesn't offer enough excitement and wind in your hair, how about a motorcycle? **Western States Motorcycle Tours,** 9401 N. Seventh Ave. (☎ **602/943-9030**), rents Harley-Davidson, BMW, and Suzuki motorcycles for between $70 and $175 per day ($400 to $750 per week). You must have a valid motorcycle driver's license to rent one of these bikes. In Arizona you don't have to wear a helmet, so you really can ride with the wind in your hair.

DRIVING RULES A right turn on a red light is permitted after a complete stop. Seat belts are required for the driver and for all passengers; children 4 years and younger, or who weigh 40 pounds or less, must be in a children's car seat. General speed limits are 25 to 35 m.p.h. in towns and cities, 15 m.p.h. in school zones, and 55 m.p.h. on two-lane highways, except rural interstate highways, where the speed limit ranges from 65 to 75 m.p.h.

If you're driving to or from other regions in Arizona, always be sure to keep your gas tank topped off. It's not unusual to drive 60 miles without seeing a gas station in many parts of Arizona. *Note:* A breakdown in the desert can be more than just an inconvenience—it can be dangerous. Always carry drinking water with you while driving through the desert, and if you plan to head off on back roads, it's a good idea to carry extra water for the car as well.

BY PUBLIC TRANSPORTATION

Unfortunately, **Valley Metro** (☎ **602/253-5000**), the Phoenix public bus system, is not very useful to tourists. It's primarily meant to be used by commuters, and most routes stop running before 9pm. For the most part, there's no bus service on Sunday, and some buses don't run on Saturday either. But if you decide you want to take the bus, pick up a copy of *The Bus Book* at one of the tourist information desks in the airport (where it's sometimes available), at Central Station at the corner of Central Avenue and Van Buren Street, or any Frys or Safeway supermarkets. There are both local and express buses. Local bus fare is $1.25, and express bus fare is $1.75. A 10-ride ticket book, all-day passes, and monthly passes are available.

Of slightly more value to visitors is the free **Downtown Area Shuttle (DASH),** which provides bus service within the downtown area. These buses operate Monday through Friday between 6:30am and 5:30pm. The buses stop at regular bus stops every 6 to 12 minutes. This shuttle is primarily for downtown workers, but attractions along the route include the state capitol, Heritage Square, and the Arizona Center shopping mall. In Tempe, **Free Local Area Shuttle (FLASH)** buses provide a similar service on a loop around Arizona State University. The route includes Mill Avenue and Sun Devil Stadium, and as the name implies, these buses are free. For information on both DASH and FLASH, call ☎ **602/253-5000.**

In Scottsdale, you can ride the **Scottsdale Round Up** (☎ **480/312-7696**) shuttle buses between Scottsdale Fashion

Square and Old Town Scottsdale. These buses operate Monday through Saturday.

BY TAXI

Because distances in Phoenix are so great, the price of an average taxi ride can be quite high. However, if you don't have your own wheels and the bus isn't running because it's late at night or the weekend, you won't have any choice but to call a cab. **Yellow Cab** (☎ **602/252-5252**) charges $3 for the first mile and $1.50 per mile after that. **Scottsdale Cab** (☎ **480/994-1616**) charges $2 per mile, with a $5 minimum.

FAST FACTS: Phoenix & Scottsdale

American Express There are American Express offices at 2508 E. Camelback Rd. (☎ **602/468-1199**), open Monday through Saturday 10am to 6pm, and at 6900 E. Camelback Rd., Scottsdale (☎ **480/949-7000**), open Monday through Friday 9:30am to 5:30pm and Saturday 9:30am to 3pm.

Airport See "Orientation," earlier in this chapter.

Baby-Sitters If your hotel can't recommend or provide a sitter, contact the **Granny Company** (☎ **602/956-4040**). For **baby equipment rentals,** such as a crib or stroller, contact Baby Boom Rentals (☎ **602/331-8881**).

Car Rentals See "Getting Around," earlier in this chapter.

Climate See "When to Go," in chapter 2.

Dentist Call **1-800-DENTIST** for a referral.

Doctor Call the **Maricopa County Medical Society** (☎ **602/252-2844**) or the **Physician Referral and Resource Line** (☎ **602/230-2273**) for doctor referrals.

Emergencies For police, fire, or medical emergency, phone ☎ **911.**

Eyeglass Repair The **Nationwide Vision Center** has more than 10 locations around the valley, including 5130 N. 19th Ave. (☎ **602/242-5293**); 3202 E. Greenway, Paradise Valley (☎ **602/788-8413**); 4615 E. Thomas Rd. (☎ **602/952-8667**); and 933 E. University Dr., Tempe (☎ **480/966-4992**).

Hospitals The **Good Samaritan Regional Medical Center,** 1111 E. McDowell Rd. (☎ **602/239-2000**), is one of the largest hospitals in the valley.

Hot Lines The **Visitor Information Line** (☎ **602/252-5588**) has recorded tourist information on Phoenix and the Valley of the Sun. **Pressline** (☎ **602/271-5656**) provides access to daily news, the correct time, weather, and other topics.

Information See "Visitor Information" under "Orientation," earlier in this chapter.

Internet Access If your hotel doesn't provide Internet access, your next best bet is to visit one of the **Kinko's** in the area. There are Kinko's locations in downtown Phoenix at 259 N. First Ave. (☎ **602/252-4055**), off the Camelback corridor at 4801 N. Central Ave. (☎ **602/241-9440**), and in Scottsdale at 4150 N. Civic Center Blvd. (☎ **480/946-0500**), and at a couple of other locations.

Lost Property If you lose something in the airport, call ☎ **602/273-3307;** on a bus, call ☎ **602/253-5000.**

Maps See "City Layout" under "Orientation," earlier in this chapter.

Newspapers & Magazines The *Arizona Republic* (www.arizonarepublic.com) is Phoenix's daily newspaper. The Thursday paper has a special section (called "The Rep") with schedules of the upcoming week's movie, music, and cultural performances. *New Times* is a free weekly news and arts journal with comprehensive listings of cultural events, film, and rock-music club and concert schedules. The best place to find *New Times* is at corner newspaper dispensers in downtown Phoenix, Scottsdale, or Tempe.

Pharmacies Call ☎ **1-800/WALGREENS** for the Walgreen's pharmacy that's nearest you; some are open 24 hours a day.

Police For police emergencies, phone ☎ **911.**

Post Office The **Phoenix Main Post Office** is at 4949 E. Van Buren St. (☎ **800/275-8777**), open Monday through Friday 8am to 5pm.

Safety Don't leave valuables in view in your car, especially when parking in downtown Phoenix. Put anything of value in the trunk, or under the seat if you're driving a hatchback. Take extra precautions after dark in the south-central Phoenix area and downtown. Violent acts of road rage are all too common in Phoenix, so it's a good idea to be polite when driving. Aggressive drivers should be given plenty of room.

Many hotels now provide in-room safes, for which there's sometimes a daily charge. Others will be glad to store your valuables in a safety-deposit box at the front office.

Taxes State sales tax is about 5% (plus variable local taxes). Hotel room taxes vary considerably by city but are mostly between 10.25% and 10.625%. However, it is in renting a car that you really get pounded. Expect to pay taxes in excess of 20% when renting a car at Sky Harbor Airport. Add to this an additional $2.50 Cactus League charge, and you end up with a considerable amount on top of the rental fee. You can save up to 10% (the airport concession fee recoupment charge) by renting your car at an office outside the airport.

Taxis See "Getting Around," earlier in this chapter.

Transit Information For **Phoenix Transit System** public bus information, call ☎ **602/253-5000.**

Weather The phone number for weather information is ☎ **602/ 271-5656,** ext. 1010.

4

Accommodations

Because the Phoenix area has long been popular as a winter refuge from cold and snow, it now has the greatest concentration of resorts in the continental United States. However, even with all the hotel rooms here, sunshine and spring training combine to make it hard to find a room on short notice between February and April (the busiest time of year in the valley). If you're planning to visit during these months, make your reservations as far in advance as possible. Also keep in mind that during the winter, the Phoenix metro area has some of the highest room rates in the country. Sure, the city has plenty of moderately priced motels, but even these places tend to jack up their prices in winter. Hotels are increasingly turning to the airline model: Rates go up and down with demand, so you never know what they might be charging on a given date. Also, don't forget that it's often possible to get a lower room rate simply by asking. If a hotel isn't full and isn't expected to be, you should be able to get a lower rate. Unfortunately, the reverse also holds true.

With the exception of valet parking services and parking garages at downtown convention hotels, parking is free at most Phoenix hotels. If there is a parking charge, we have noted it. You'll find that all hotels have no-smoking rooms and all but the cheapest have wheelchair-accessible rooms.

Also, keep in mind that most resorts offer a variety of weekend, golf, and tennis packages, as well as special off-season discounts and corporate rates (which you can often get just by asking). We've given only the official "rack rates," or walk-in rates, below, but it always pays to ask if there's any kind of special discount or package available. Don't forget your ACCOMMODATIONS or AARP discounts if you belong to these organizations. (If you aren't already a member, it's worth joining just to get the discounts.) Also keep in mind that business hotels downtown and near the airport often lower their rates on weekends.

If you're looking to save some money, consider traveling during the shoulder seasons of late spring and late summer. Temperatures are not at their midsummer peak nor are room rates at their midwinter highs. (And if you can stand the heat of summer, you can often save more than 50% on room rates.) If you'll be traveling with children, always ask whether your child will be able to stay for free in your room, and whether there's a limit to the number of children who can stay for free.

Request a room with a view of the mountains whenever possible. You can overlook a swimming pool anywhere, but some of the main selling points of Phoenix and Scottsdale hotels are the views of Mummy Mountain, Camelback Mountain, and Squaw Peak.

BED & BREAKFAST INNS While most people dreaming of an Arizona winter vacation have visions of luxury resorts dancing in their heads, there are also plenty of bed-and-breakfast inns around the valley. **Advance Reservations Inn Arizona/Mi Casa-Su Casa Bed & Breakfast Reservation Service,** P.O. Box 950, Tempe, AZ 85280-0950 (☎ **800/456-0682** or 480/990-0682; www.azres.com), can book you into more than 65 homes in the Valley of the Sun, as can **Arizona Trails Bed & Breakfast Reservation Service,** P.O. Box 18998, Fountain Hills, AZ 85269-8998 (☎ **888/799-4284** or 480/837-4284; fax 480/816-4224; www.arizonatrails.com), which also books tour and hotel reservations.

PRICE CATEGORIES Because it is such a popular winter resort destination, Phoenix is one of the more expensive places in the United States for a vacation. If you've been thinking of saving money by skipping the Caribbean or Hawaii this year, think again. When a standard room at a top resort goes for well over $250 and a Super 8 Motel charges close to $100, price categories become very subjective. Consequently, we have categorized accommodations based on their relative cost when compared with other Valley of the Sun accommodations.

Phoenix, Scottsdale & the Valley of the Sun Accommodations

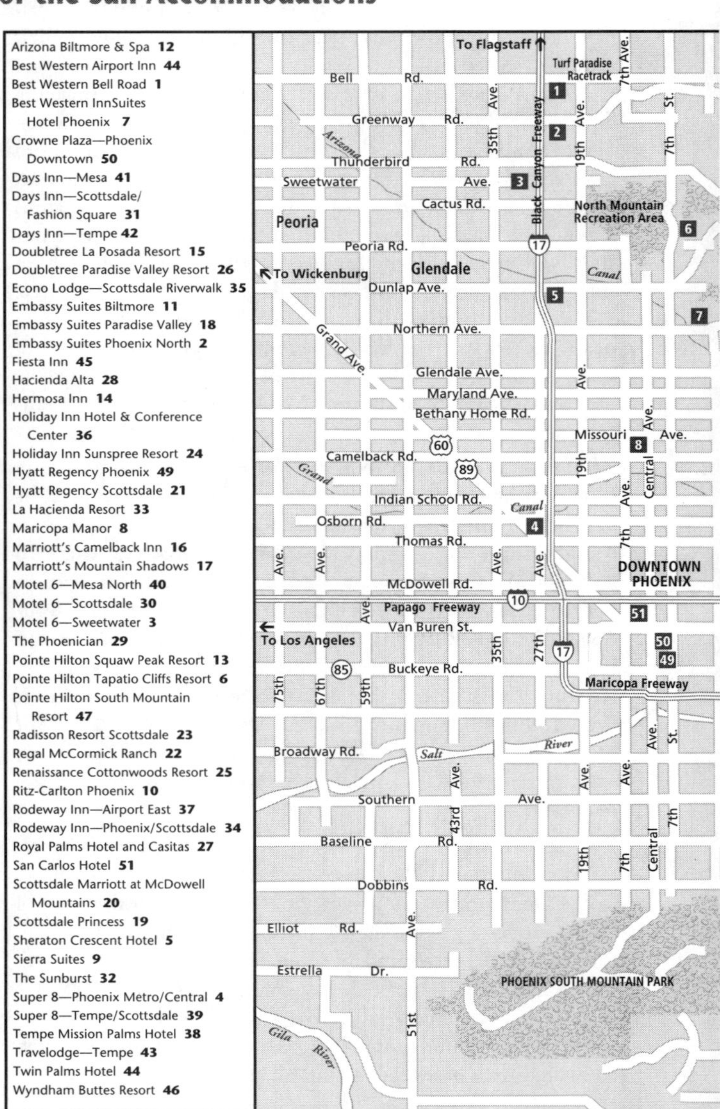

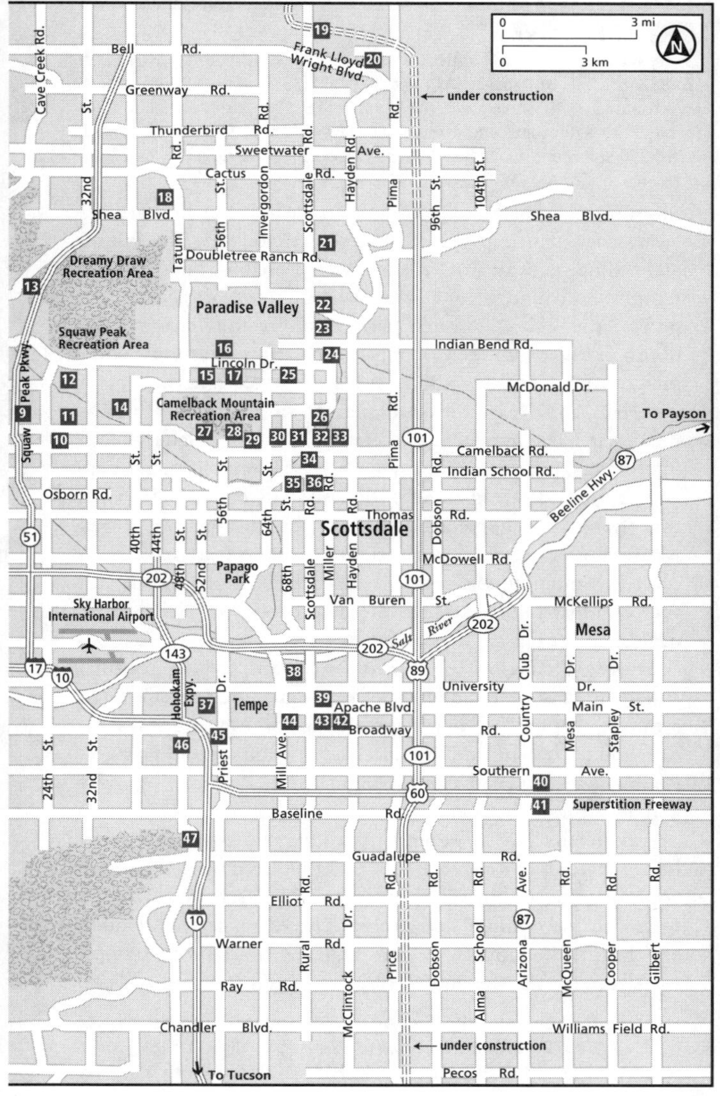
0
3 mi
0
3 km
N
under construction
Bell
Rd.
Frank Lloyd Wright Blvd.
Cave Creek Rd.
Greenway
Rd.
Thunderbird
Rd.
Sweetwater
Ave.
Cactus
Rd.
Shea
Blvd.
Shea
Blvd.
32nd
St.
Tatum
56th
St.
Invergordon
Rd.
Scottsdale
Rd.
Hayden
Rd.
Pima
Rd.
96th
St.
104th
St.
Dreamy Draw Recreation Area
Doubletree Ranch Rd.
Paradise Valley
Squaw Peak Recreation Area
Squaw Peak Pkwy.
Lincoln Dr.
Indian Bend Rd.
McDonald Dr.
To Payson
Camelback Mountain Recreation Area
Camelback Rd.
Indian School Rd.
Beeline Hwy.
Osborn Rd.
Thomas
Rd.
Scottsdale
40th
44th
48th
52nd
64th
68th
Miller
Dobson
McDowell
Rd.
Papago Park
Sky Harbor International Airport
Van
Buren
St.
McKellips
Rd.
Salt River
Mesa
Hohokam Expy.
Tempe
University
Dr.
Apache Blvd.
Main
St.
Broadway
Rd.
Club
Country
Mesa
Stapley
Priest
Mill Ave.
24th
St.
32nd
St.
Southern
Ave.
Baseline
Rd.
Superstition Freeway
Guadalupe
Rd.
Elliot
Rd.
Warner
Rd.
Rural
McClintock
Price
Dobson
School
Alma
Arizona
Ave.
McQueen
Cooper
Gilbert
Ray
Rd.
Chandler
Blvd.
Williams
Field
Rd.
under construction
To Tucson
Pecos
Rd.
1
2
3
4
5
6
7
8
9
10
11
12
13
14
15
16
17
18
19
20
21
22
23
24
25
26
27
28
29
30
31
32
33
34
35
36
37
38
39
40
41
42
43
44
45
46
47
17
10
51
202
143
101
87
89
60

1 Scottsdale

VERY EXPENSIVE

✪ **Hyatt Regency Scottsdale.** 7500 E. Doubletree Ranch Rd., Scottsdale, AZ 85258. ☎ **800/55-HYATT** or 480/991-3388. Fax 480/483-5550. www.hyatt.com. 493 units. A/C MINIBAR TV TEL. Jan–late May $375–$500 double, from $900 suites and casitas; late May–early Sept $155–$305 double, from $250 suites and casitas; early Sept–Dec $330–$460 double, from $500 suites and casitas. AE, CB, DC, DISC, JCB, MC, V.

From the colonnades of palm trees to the lobby walls that slide away, this luxurious resort is designed to astonish. Future archaeologists excavating the site will probably think it was a temple. Surrounded by a lake, gardens, fountains, and fishponds, the 2½-acre water playground is the resort's focal point. This extravagant complex of 10 swimming pools includes a waterslide, a sand beach, a water-volleyball pool, waterfalls, and a huge whirlpool spa. (You'd never know this was the desert.) The resort's Hopi Learning Center, staffed by Hopi interpreters, provides a glimpse into Native American culture.

The grounds are planted with hundreds of tall palm trees that frame the gorgeous views of the distant McDowell Mountains; closer at hand, original works of art have been placed throughout the resort. Guest rooms are luxurious and very comfortable and reflect the desert location. Robes, hair dryers, and scales are all standard.

Dining/Diversions: The Golden Swan, serving regional American cuisine, includes a popular waterside terrace dining area (see chapter 5). There's also a casual Southwestern restaurant and an Italian cafe that offers after-dinner gondola rides. A lobby bar features live music nightly. There are also two bars and a grill near the pool.

Amenities: Twenty-seven outstanding holes of golf (with lots of water hazards), 10 pools, eight tennis courts, a croquet court, jogging and bicycling trails, and a full-service health spa with exercise equipment, aerobics classes, saunas, and body and beauty treatments. A concierge, 24-hour room service, valet/laundry service, and children's programs are available.

✪ **Marriott's Camelback Inn.** 5402 E. Lincoln Dr., Scottsdale, AZ 85253. ☎ **800/24-CAMEL** or 480/948-1700. Fax 480/951-8469. www.camelbackinn.com. 453 units. A/C MINIBAR TV TEL. Jan to mid-May $329–$419 double, $515–$2,050 suite; mid-May to early Sept $159–$295 double, $215–$1,525 suite; early Sept–Dec $255–$329 double, $395–$1,550 suite. AE, CB, DC, DISC, EC, JCB, MC, V. Small pets accepted.

Set at the foot of Mummy Mountain and overlooking Camelback Mountain, the Camelback Inn, which opened in 1936, is one of the grande dames of the Phoenix hotel scene. Over the past few years it has undergone $35 million worth of renovations, yet the resort still retains its traditional Southwestern character and solid sense of place. Although the two 18-hole golf courses are the main attractions for many guests here, the spa is among the finest in the state, and there's an extensive pool complex that appeals to families. The guest rooms, which are spread out over the sloping grounds, are decorated with contemporary Southwestern furnishings and art, and all have balconies or patios.

Dining/Diversions: The Chaparral serves new American cuisine in a relaxed atmosphere, while the Navajo Room is more casual. Healthy meals are served at the spa's restaurant. There are also two snack bars, a lounge for cocktails, and a cafe for espresso and pastries.

Amenities: Two outstanding 18-hole golf courses, a pitch-and-putt course, six tennis courts, three pools, three whirlpools, a playground, basketball and volleyball courts, one of the best full-service health spas in the valley, concierge, room service, baby-sitting, children's programs, valet/laundry service, and a car-rental desk.

✪ **The Phoenician.** 6000 E. Camelback Rd., Scottsdale, AZ 85251. ☎ **800/888-8234** or 480/941-8200. Fax 480/947-4311. www.thephoenician. com. 654 units. A/C MINIBAR TV TEL. Late Dec to mid-May $525–$655 double, $1,350–$5,500 suite; mid-May to early June $435–$485 double, $1,224–$5,500 suite; early June to mid-Sept $195–$245 double, $500–$5,300 suite; mid-Sept to late Dec $435–$485 double, $1,225–$5,500 suite. AE, CB, DC, DISC, MC, V. Valet parking $18. Pets under 25 lbs. accepted.

The Phoenician consistently ranks among the finest resorts in the world, and no expense was spared in the construction of the palatial resort, which is situated on 250 acres at the foot of Camelback Mountain. Polished marble and sparkling crystal abound in the lobby, but the view of the valley through a long wall of glass is what commands most guests' attention. Service here is second to none, and the pool complex is one of the finest in the state. The resort's spa offers all the pampering anyone could ever need, and there are also 27 challenging holes of golf.

Guest rooms are as elaborate as the public areas and include sunken bathtubs for two, Berber carpets, three phones, large patios, terry robes, bathroom scales, hair dryers, and wall safes. And that's just the *standard* room. The separate Canyon Building has its own private pool complete with rental cabanas.

Dining/Diversions: Mary Elaine's, Phoenix's ultimate special-occasion restaurant, features modern French cuisine and great views. The Terrace Dining Room serves Italian and is less formal, while Windows on the Green features Southwestern cuisine with a golf course view. There are also poolside snack bars. Afternoon tea in the lobby is also very popular and posh.

Amenities: In addition to the golf course and full-service spa, there are nine pools (including one lined with opalescent tiles), a waterslide, a putting green, 11 tennis courts, a whirlpool, lawn games, rental bikes, and a shopping arcade. Also available are a car-rental desk, business center, concierge, 24-hour room service, valet/laundry service, baby-sitting, and children's programs.

Regal McCormick Ranch Resort & Villas. 7401 N. Scottsdale Rd., Scottsdale, AZ 85253-3548. ☎ **800/222-8888** or 480/948-5050. Fax 480/991-5572. www.regal-hotels.com. 179 units. A/C MINIBAR TV TEL. Jan 1–Apr 30 $219–$299 double, from $360 suite or villa; May 1–May 31 $149–$199 double, from $274 suite or villa; June 1 to mid-Sept $109–$149 double, from $224 suite or villa; mid-Sept to Dec 31 $169–$219 double, from $294 suite or villa. AE, CB, DC, DISC, MC, V.

Surrounded by green lawns, a golf course, and a lake, this relatively small resort strives to convince you that you're not in the desert. The lake (complete with sailboats for guests) is the focal point, but more traditional resort activities are available at the two 18-hole golf courses and on the three tennis courts. The guest rooms all have their own private balconies or patios, and more than half the rooms overlook the lake. If you're here with your family, consider the spacious villas. So if you like the heat but not the desert, this resort, with its lakefront setting, is a good bet.

Dining/Diversions: The resort's restaurant serves good Southwestern fare, and there is an adjacent bar and grill. Both have views of the lake.

Amenities: Two 18-hole golf courses, outdoor pool overlooking lake, three lighted tennis courts (and pro shop, lessons, and clinics), whirlpool, walking/jogging paths, concierge, room service, valet/laundry service.

Renaissance Scottsdale Resort. 6160 N. Scottsdale Rd., Scottsdale, AZ 85253. ☎ **800/HOTELS-1** or 480/991-1414. Fax 480/951-3350. www.renaissancehotels.com. 171 units. A/C MINIBAR TV TEL. Jan to mid-May $210–$229 double, $259–$325 suite; Mid-May to early Sept $75 double, $99–$105 suite; early Sept–Dec $75–189 double, $99–$285 suite. AE, DC, DISC, MC, V. Pets under 25 lbs. accepted ($50 deposit).

Located behind the upscale Borgata shopping center (which is designed to resemble an Italian village), the Renaissance Scottsdale Resort is an unpretentious-yet-luxurious boutique resort. Set amid shady lawns, the resort consists of spacious suites designed for those who need plenty of room and comfort. More than 100 of the suites have their own private hot tubs on private patios, and all the suites are done in Southwestern style. Several excellent restaurants are within walking distance, which makes this a good choice for gourmands who don't want to spend their vacation fighting rush-hour traffic on Scottsdale Road.

Dining/Diversions: The resort's restaurant and lounge are in a separate building (in front of the Borgata). There's also a poolside bar.

Amenities: Around the resort's spacious grounds you'll find two swimming pools, two hot tubs, four tennis courts, a jogging trail, putting green, and a croquet lawn. There are also bicycles for guests and access to a nearby health club (for an additional charge). A concierge, room service, and valet service are all available.

✪ **The Sunburst Resort.** 4925 N. Scottsdale Rd., Scottsdale, AZ 85251. ☎ **800/528-7867** or 480/945-7666. Fax 480/946-4056. www.sunburstresort.com. 210 units. A/C MINIBAR TV TEL. Jan to mid-Apr $235–$285 double, $635–$950 suite; mid-Apr to mid-May $215–$255 double, $575–$850 suite; late May to mid-Sept $95–$135 double, $300–$450 suite; mid-Sept to Dec $185–$225 double, $500–$750 suite. AE, CB, DC, DISC, MC, V.

An exceptional location in the heart of the Scottsdale shopping district, a dramatic Southwestern styling, and a small but well-designed pool area are the primary appeals of this resort. The focal point of the lobby is a massive sandstone fireplace; in the resort's lushly planted courtyard is a small lagoon-style pool complete with sand beach, short waterslide, and flame-topped columnar waterfalls. An artificial stream, waterfalls, and fake sandstone ruins all add up to a fun desert fantasy landscape (although not on the grand scale to be found at some area resorts).

Guest rooms are comfortable and decorated in new "Old West" styling, with cowhide prints and peeled log furnishings. Bathrooms have double vanities, and French doors open onto patios.

Dining/Diversions: The resort's dining room features a mix of Mediterranean and Southwestern flavors. There's also a lobby bar.

Amenities: Pools, whirlpool, fitness room, concierge, room service, and valet/laundry. There's no golf course, but tee times can be arranged at nearby courses.

EXPENSIVE

Doubletree La Posada Resort. 4949 E. Lincoln Dr., Scottsdale, AZ 85253. ☎ **800/222-TREE** or 602/952-0420. Fax 602/840-8576. www.laposadaresort.com. 262 units. A/C MINIBAR TV TEL. Mid-Sept to mid-May $140–$200 double, $400–$550 suite; mid-May to mid-Sept $79–$112 double, $400–$550 suite. AE, CB, DC, DISC, MC, V.

If you prefer to spend your time by the pool rather than on the fairways, La Posada is a great choice, especially if you have the kids along. The pool here, which has a view of Camelback Mountain, covers half an acre and features its own two-story waterfall that cascades over artificial boulders. Connecting the two halves of the pool is a swim-through grotto complete with bar/cafe (and fitness room).

Mission-revival architecture prevails throughout the resort. The guest rooms are larger than average and have tiled bathrooms with a double vanity.

Dining/Diversions: The Garden Terrace restaurant has a nice view of Camelback Mountain and offers somewhat pricey Southwestern cuisine (although Sunday brunch is a great deal by Phoenix standards). There's also an adjacent lounge, as well as a poolside grill.

Amenities: In addition to facilities mentioned above, there are tennis and racquetball courts, two putting greens, four whirlpools, a fitness room, a volleyball court, and a tennis pro shop. A car-rental desk, concierge, room service, and laundry/valet service are also available.

✪ **Doubletree Paradise Valley Resort.** 5401 N. Scottsdale Rd., Scottsdale, AZ 85250. ☎ **800/222-TREE** or 480/947-5400. Fax 480/481-0209. www.doubletreehotels.com. 387 units. A/C MINIBAR TV TEL. Sept–May $175–$335 double, from $300 suite; May–Aug $85–$145 double, from $189 suite. AE, CB, DC, DISC, MC, V.

This resort gives a bow to the pioneering architectural style of Frank Lloyd Wright, and thus stands out from other comparable Scottsdale resorts. Built around several courtyards containing swimming pools, bubbling fountains, and desert gardens, the resort has much the look and feel of the Hyatt Regency (although on a less grandiose scale). Mature palm trees lend a sort of Moorish feel to the grounds and cast fanciful shadows in the gardens.

Guest rooms have a very contemporary feel, with lots of blond wood, and, in some cases, high ceilings that make the rooms feel particularly spacious. There are also large closets and separate dressing rooms and bathrooms, and coffeemakers, hair dryers, and irons/ironing boards are standard.

Dining/Diversions: A skylit dining room serves Southwestern dishes, while grilled meals are available on an adjacent patio. A lobby lounge serves drinks and light meals, often to the accompaniment of live music. There's also a poolside bar.

Amenities: Two outdoor pools (set in palm-shaded courtyards and with small waterfalls), tennis and racquetball courts, a fitness center, putting green, saunas, whirlpools, business center, car-rental desk, concierge, room service, valet/laundry service, baby-sitting.

Embassy Suites Paradise Valley at Stonecreek Golf Club. 4415 E. Paradise Village Pkwy. S., Paradise Valley, AZ 85032. ☎ **800/EMBASSY** or 602/569-0888. Fax 602/569-1308. www.embassysuitesaz.com. 270 units. A/C TV TEL. Oct–Apr $159–$199 double; May–June $129–$169 double; July–Sept $109–$149 double. Rates include full breakfast. AE, CB, DC, DISC, JCB, MC, V.

While cities from New York to San Francisco are busy opening chic and stylishly contemporary hotels as fast as they can, the Valley of the Sun has nearly missed the boat completely. That is, until this Embassy Suites opened in 2000. As soon as you see the dyed concrete floor and unusual wall sculpture in the lobby, you'll know that this is not your standard business hotel. However, it might be difficult to take your eyes off the views across Stonecreek Golf Course to Camelback Mountain, Mummy Mountain, and Squaw Peak, and those views just get better the higher up you go in the hotel (be sure to ask for a room on the south side of an upper floor). Keep in mind that this is an all-suite property, and the two-room accommodations are very spacious and have galley kitchens.

Dining/Diversions: The hotel's dining room overlooks the driving range and serves contemporary American dishes. There's also an adjacent lounge and a nightly complimentary cocktail reception.

Amenities: Pool, whirlpool, fitness room, room service, concierge, valet/laundry service.

Marriott's Mountain Shadows Resort & Golf Club. 5641 E. Lincoln Dr., Scottsdale, AZ 85253. ☎ **800/228-9290** or 480/948-7111. Fax 480/951-5430. 337 units. A/C MINIBAR TV TEL. Jan to mid-May $179–$199 double, $305–$700 suite; mid-May to early Sept $69–$149 double, $135–$415 suite; early Sept–Dec $149–$199 double, $265–$650 suite. AE, CB, DC, DISC, JCB, MC, V. Small pets accepted.

Located across the road from Marriott's Camelback Inn, Mountain Shadows offers better views of Camelback Mountain and an entirely different ambience. Mountain Shadows, built in the late 1950s and architecturally dated, is, however, well maintained and will appeal to anyone looking for an informal atmosphere. An 18-hole executive course keeps most guests happy, but guests can also use the Camelback Inn's courses (and its superb spa).

Standard rooms are large and have high ceilings, wet bars, king-size beds, and balconies. The rooms around the main pool, although large, can be a bit noisy. Those rooms in the Palm section offer the best views of the mountain.

Dining/Diversions: There's a seafood restaurant and a more casual Southwest-style cafe, as well as a bar and grill, a country club dining room, and a poolside snack bar.

Amenities: In addition to the golf course, there are eight tennis courts, three pools (one of which is quite large), two whirlpools, a fitness center, a volleyball court, pro shops, a business center, concierge, room service, valet/laundry service, car-rental desk, baby-sitting, children's programs, and guided mountain hikes.

Radisson Resort Scottsdale. 7171 N. Scottsdale Rd., Scottsdale, AZ 85253. ☎ **800/333-3333** or 480/991-3800. Fax 480/948-1381. www.radisson.com/scottsdaleaz. 318 units. A/C TV TEL. Mid-Jan to late May $139–$299 double, $359–$1,500 suite; late May–late June $175–$199 double, $295–$1,500 suite; late June to mid-Sept $125–$149 double, $199–$1,500 suite; mid-Sept to mid-Jan $220–$245 double, $325–$1,500 suite. AE, CB, DC, DISC, JCB, MC, V.

With all its green lawns and big trees, this resort feels far more Midwestern than southwestern, but if you want greenery and a conservative atmosphere, this is a good bet. Most guests are attracted by the resort's 21 tennis courts or two 18-hole golf courses. A large Japanese-style health spa rounds out the resort amenities here. Most rooms are large and have comfortable chairs and private patios, but the golf-course rooms, with their views of the McDowell Mountains, are our favorites.

Dining/Diversions: There's a rather formal dining room serving new American fare, a spa restaurant, a pub, a poolside snack bar, and even a tiny patisserie.

Amenities: In addition to the golf, tennis, and spa facilities, you'll find a pro shop, three pools, whirlpool, a health club ($15 charge), a concierge, room service, valet/laundry service, a car-rental desk.

MODERATE

Holiday Inn Hotel & Conference Center. 7353 E. Indian School Rd., Scottsdale, AZ 85251. ☎ **800/695-6995** or 480/994-9203. Fax 480/941-2567. www.holidayinnscottsdale.com. 206 units. A/C TV TEL. Mid-Jan to mid-Apr $105–$165 double, from $250 suite; mid-Apr to late May $89–$129 double, from $189 suite; late May–early Sept $50–$90 double, from $145 suite; early Sept–Dec 31 $89–$129 double, from $189 suite. AE, CB, DC, DISC, JCB, MC, V. Pets accepted.

Guest rooms at this low-rise hotel in Old Town Scottsdale are fairly small (as are the bathrooms), but the location right on the beautifully landscaped Scottsdale Civic Center Mall (a park, not a shopping center) is very appealing. You're only a block off Scottsdale's famous shopping and gallery neighborhood, and the Scottsdale Center for the Arts is just across the mall. The best rooms are those opening onto the mall—be sure to request one. The hotel's dining room is a very economical steakhouse overlooking the park. There's also a lively lounge, small outdoor pool, tennis court, whirlpool, putting, baby-sitting, room service, and shopping shuttle.

✪ **Holiday Inn SunSpree Resort.** 7601 E. Indian Bend Rd., Scottsdale, AZ 85250. ☎ **800/852-5205** or 480/991-2400. Fax 480/998-2261. www.holiday-inn.com/scottsdale-rst. 200 units. A/C TV TEL. Oct–late Apr $119–$190 double; late Apr–late May $99–$170 double; late May–Sept $59–$100 double. AE, CB, DC, DISC, JCB, MC, V.

During the winter and spring, it's almost impossible to find a reasonably priced resort in Scottsdale, but this attractive and economical hotel fits the bill. Situated on 16 acres amid wide expanses of lawn, the SunSpree Resort certainly is not as luxurious as most other area resorts, but with its relatively low rates and policy of allowing kids under 12 to eat free in the resort's main restaurants, this is a good choice for families (the adjacent McCormick-Stillman Railroad Park is also a big hit with kids). Guest rooms have a plush feel that belies the economical rates. Ask for a mountain view or lakeside room with a patio. There's a restaurant overlooking the lake, as well as a lobby lounge and poolside bar, and room service is available. In addition to a swimming pool and whirlpool, the resort has a fitness room, tennis, volleyball, croquet, and horseshoes.

La Hacienda Resort. 7320 E. Camelback Rd., Scottsdale, AZ 85251. ☎ **480/994-4170.** www.suitedreamsaz.com. 22 units. Mid-Nov to late May $99–$149 double, $159–$279 suite; mid-May to Dec 31 $79–$89 double, $109–$179 suite. AE, MC, V. Pets accepted.

Don't be taken in by the name; this little place is hardly a resort, but it is a well-placed and well-priced getaway spot with the look and feel of an updated 1960s apartment court. Funky and hip are the watchwords here, although the hipness is mostly in the tiny lobby, which has decoupaged walls, faux-painted floors, and an espresso machine. The inn's grassy little courtyard, which has a small pool and a hot tub, is set off from busy Camelback Road by a brick wall that gives the complex a private, residential feel. Rooms are fairly well maintained and range from big to huge. Although the bathrooms are small, most rooms have full kitchens. Within just a few blocks are lots of nightclubs, great restaurants, and excellent shopping. This hotel is a good choice for younger travelers.

INEXPENSIVE

Despite the high-priced real estate, Scottsdale does have a few relatively inexpensive chain motels, although during the winter season prices are higher than you'd expect. The rates given here are for the high season: The **Days Inn—Scottsdale/Fashion Square Resort,** 4710 N. Scottsdale Rd. (☎ **480/947-5411**), charging $79 to $130 double; **Motel 6—Scottsdale,** 6848 E. Camelback Rd. (☎ **480/946-2280**), charging $72 double; and **Rodeway Inn—Phoenix/Scottsdale,** 7110 E. Indian School Rd. (☎ **480/946-3456**), charging $63 to $120 double.

Econo Lodge-Scottsdale Riverwalk. 6935 Fifth Ave., Scottsdale, AZ 85251. ☎ **800/55-ECONO** or 480/994-9461. Fax 480/947-1695. www.choicehotels.com. 92 units. A/C TV TEL. Oct 1 to mid-Apr $69–$109 double; mid-Apr to

June 30 $59–$99 double; July 1–Sept 30 $49–$89 double. Rates include continental breakfast. AE, CB, DC, DISC, JCB, MC, V.

For convenience and price, this motel can't be beat (at least not in Scottsdale). Located at the west end of the Fifth Avenue shopping district, this motel is within walking distance of some of the best shopping and dining in Scottsdale. The guest rooms are large and have been recently renovated. The three-story building is arranged around a central courtyard where you'll find the pool. Local phone calls are free, and there's a fitness room.

2 North Scottsdale, Carefree & Cave Creek

VERY EXPENSIVE

✪ **The Boulders.** 34631 N. Tom Darlington Dr. (P.O. Box 2090), Carefree, AZ 85377. ☎ **800/553-1717,** 888/472-6229, or 480/488-9009. Fax 480/488-4118. www.grandbay.com. 160 casitas. A/C MINIBAR TV TEL. Mid-Jan to late Apr $565 double, from $765 villa; early to mid-Jan, late Apr–late May, and early Sept to early Dec $450 double, from $625 villa; late May–early June and mid-Dec $265 double, from $425 villa; mid-June to early Sept $185 double, from $415 villa (all rates plus $20 to $24 nightly service charge). AE, CB, DC, DISC, MC, V. Pets accepted ($100 refundable deposit).

Set amid a jumble of giant boulders 45 minutes north of Scottsdale, this resort epitomizes the Southwest aesthetic and is the state's premier golf resort. Adobe buildings blend unobtrusively into the desert, as do the two noted golf courses, which feature the most breathtaking tee boxes in Arizona. If you can tear yourself away from the fairways, you can relax around either of two pools, play tennis (no boulders on the courts), or take advantage of the full-service spa. The distance from Scottsdale is this resort's only real shortcoming.

The lobby is an organic adobe structure with tree-trunk pillars, a flagstone floor, and a collection of Native American artifacts on display. The guest rooms continue the adobe styling with stucco walls, beehive fireplaces, and beamed ceilings. The bathrooms are large and luxuriously appointed with tubs for two, separate showers, double vanities, and hair dryers. The best views are from second-floor rooms.

Dining/Diversions: The Latilla Room, the resort's premier restaurant, serves innovative American cuisine. The Palo Verde Room is a more casual spot serving Southwestern dishes. There's also a country club dining room, and, in the resort's

El Pedregal Marketplace, several other dining options. A comfortable lounge features live jazz in the evenings.

Amenities: Two 18-hole golf courses, full-service spa, fitness center, six tennis courts, three pools, jogging and hiking trails, pro shop, rental bikes, concierge, room service, valet/laundry service, baby-sitting, children's programs (holidays only), rock-climbing program.

The Fairmont Scottsdale Princess. 7575 E. Princess Dr., Scottsdale, AZ 85255. ☎ **800/344-4758** or 480/585-4848. Fax 480/585-0086. www.fairmont.com. 650 units. A/C MINIBAR TV TEL. $149–$539 double; $309–$3,500 suite. AE, CB, DC, DISC, MC, V.

With its royal palms, tiled fountains, waterfalls, and classical art and antiques, the Princess is a modern rendition of a Moorish palace and offers a truly exotic atmosphere unmatched by any other valley resort. It's also home to the Phoenix Open golf tournament and the city's top tennis tournament, which means the two golf courses here are superb and the courts are top-notch. For those not tempted by golf or tennis, there's a full-service spa and fitness center. This resort, which is located a 20-minute drive north of Old Scottsdale, will delight anyone in search of a romantic hideaway.

The guest room decor is elegant Southwestern, and all the rooms have private balconies. The spacious bathrooms have double vanities and a separate shower and tub. For more space, there's a wide variety of suites available.

Dining/Diversions: The Marquesa serves superb (and expensive) Spanish cuisine, while upscale Mexican and strolling mariachis are the specialties at La Hacienda. See chapter 5 for more information on these two restaurants. There are a couple of casual restaurants and, at the golf course, a steakhouse. For drinks you'll find a quiet lounge and a rowdy Wild West saloon.

Amenities: In addition to the two 18-hole golf courses, there are seven tennis courts; three pools; whirlpools; racquetball, squash, and basketball courts; a fitness trail; a complete spa and fitness center; boutiques; tennis and golf pro shops; and a business center. There's even a fishing pond here (which kids love). A concierge, 24-hour room service, valet/laundry service, baby-sitting, and shopping shuttle are also available.

Four Seasons Resort Scottsdale at Troon North. 10600 E. Crescent Moon Dr., Scottsdale, AZ 85255. ☎ **800/332-3442** or 480/515-5700. Fax 480/515-5599. www.fourseasons.com. 210 units. A/C MINIBAR TV TEL. Mid-Dec to mid-May $475–625 double, $850–$3,500 suite; mid-May to mid-June and mid-Sept to mid-Dec $395–$495 double, $850–$3,500 suite; mid-June to mid-Sept $250–$300 double, $475–$3,500 suite. AE, DC, DISC, JCB, MC, V. Pets accepted.

With the late 1999 opening of this Four Seasons Resort, the valley resort scene got cranked up yet another notch on the luxury accommodations scale. Located in the foothills of north Scottsdale and adjacent to the Troon North golf course (one of the state's most highly acclaimed courses), the Four Seasons is working hard to knock The Boulders from its pinnacle. With casita accommodations scattered across a boulder-strewn hillside, the Four Seasons can certainly boast one of the most dramatic settings in the valley. Likewise, the guest rooms and suites are among the most spacious and luxurious you'll find in Arizona. If you can afford it, opt for one of the suites with an outdoor shower (a luxury usually found only in tropical resorts) and private plunge pool.

Dining/Diversions: With three restaurants on the premises, it's easy to forget how far out of the Scottsdale mainstream you are up here. There's a formal dining room serving new American fare, a more casual bistro serving Italian and California-style dishes, and a poolside bar/cafe serving lighter fare. There's also a lobby lounge.

Amenities: Large two-level pool, whirlpool, children's pool, four tennis courts, large fitness center (instructors available), full-service health spa, 24-hour room service, concierge, valet/laundry service, overnight shoeshine, children's programs.

EXPENSIVE

Scottsdale Marriott at McDowell Mountains. 16770 N. Perimeter Dr., Scottsdale, AZ 85260. ☎ **800/228-9290** or 480/502-3836. Fax 480/502-0653. www.marriottscottsdale.com. 270 units. A/C TV TEL. Jan to mid-May $229–$289 double; mid-May to mid-Sept $99–$209 double; mid-Sept to Dec $189–$209 double. AE, DC, DISC, JCB, MC, V.

This new all-suite resort, not far from the Scottsdale Princess, overlooks the Tournament Players Club (TPC) Desert Course. While this may not be the TPC's main course, it still manages to give this hotel a very resort-like feel. Suites provide lots of space and have luxurious bathrooms done in marble and granite. Some suites have balconies, and those overlooking the golf course are worth requesting, although there are also good views of the McDowell Mountains from some rooms.

Dining/Diversions: The hotel's Zambra Grille serves Mediterranean food, and there's also a lounge serving tapas. Poolside, there's a bar and grill.

Amenities: Pool, whirlpool, sauna, fitness room, room service, concierge, guest laundry, valet service.

3 Central Phoenix & the Camelback Corridor

VERY EXPENSIVE

✪ **Arizona Biltmore Resort & Spa.** 24th St. and Missouri Ave., Phoenix, AZ 85016. ☎ **800/950-0086** or 602/955-6600. Fax 602/954-2571. www.arizonabiltmore.com. 730 units. A/C TV TEL. Early Sept–Dec and early May to mid-June $295–$420 double, from $420 suite; Jan 1–early May $330–$495 double, from $650 suite; mid-June to early Sept, $165–$245 double, from $340 suite (all rates plus $12 daily service fee). AE, CB, DC, DISC, EC, JCB, MC, V. Pets under 15 lbs. accepted in cottage rooms with $250 deposit, $50 nonrefundable.

For timeless elegance, a prime location, and historic character, no other resort in the valley can touch the Arizona Biltmore. For decades this has been the favored Phoenix address of celebrities and politicians, and the distinctive cast-cement blocks designed by Frank Lloyd Wright make it one of the valley's architectural gems. What this all means is that the Biltmore is *the* Phoenix address for those who can afford to stay where they want. While the two golf courses are the main draws for many guests, the children's activities center makes it a popular choice for families. Biltmore Fashion Park shopping center is also nearby.

Of the several different styles of accommodations, the "resort rooms" are the largest and most comfortable and have balconies or patios. The rooms in the Arizona Wing, added in 1999, are also good choices. The villa suites are the Biltmore's most spacious and luxurious accommodations.

Dining/Diversions: Wright's offers a formal setting and serves excellent new American cuisine amid the handiwork of Frank Lloyd Wright. The Biltmore Grill serves meals with a touch of the Southwest both in flavors and decor. There's a quiet lobby/terrace bar and a poolside bar/restaurant. Afternoon tea, a Phoenix institution, is served in the lobby.

Amenities: Two 18-hole golf courses, 18-hole putting course, a full-service spa, five swimming pools (including one with a waterslide and one with rental cabanas), two whirlpool spas, seven lighted tennis courts, fitness center, sauna, steam room, jogging paths, rental bicycles, lawn games, business center, shops, concierge, room service, courtesy car, valet/ laundry service, car-rental service.

Hermosa Inn. 5532 N. Palo Cristi Rd., Paradise Valley, AZ 85253. ☎ **800/ 241-1210** or 602/955-8614. Fax 602/955-8299. www.hermosainn.com. 35 units. A/C TV TEL. Early Jan–early May $260–$330 double, $435–$635 suite; early May–late May $170–$210 double, $435–$520 suite; late May to mid-Sept $95–$140 double, $300–$450 suite; early Sept–early Jan $220–$275 double, $400–$550 suite. Rates include continental breakfast. AE, CB, DC, DISC, MC, V. Take 32nd St. north from Camelback Rd., turn right on Stanford Rd., and then turn left on N. Palo Cristi Rd. From Lincoln Dr., turn south on N. Palo Christi Rd. (east of 32nd St.). Pets under 20 lbs. accepted with $250 deposit, $50 nonrefundable.

This luxurious boutique hotel, once a guest ranch, is now one of the only hotels in the Phoenix area to offer a bit of Old Arizona atmosphere. Originally built in 1930 as the home of Western artist Lon Megargee, the inn is situated in a quiet residential neighborhood on more than 6 acres of neatly landscaped gardens. If you don't like the crowds of big resorts, but do enjoy the luxury, this is the spot for you.

Rooms here vary from cozy to spacious and are individually decorated in tastefully contemporary Western and Southwestern decor that would look at home on the pages of any interior design magazine. The largest suites, which have more Southwestern flavor than just about any other rooms in the area, incorporate a mixture of contemporary and antique Southwestern furnishings and accent pieces.

Dining/Diversions: Lon's, the hotel's dining room, is named for the hotel's original owner and is located in the original adobe home. Excellent new American and Southwestern cuisine is served in the rustic, upscale setting. See chapter 5 for more information.

Amenities: Small outdoor pool, two whirlpools, three tennis courts, concierge.

The Ritz-Carlton Phoenix. 2401 E. Camelback Rd., Phoenix, AZ 85016. ☎ **800/241-3333** or 602/468-0700. Fax 602/468-9883. 281 units. A/C MINIBAR TV TEL. Early Sept to mid-May $325–$375 double, $375–$425 suite; mid-May to early Sept $199–$249 double, $249–$299 suite. AE, CB, DC, DISC, MC, V. Valet parking $18.

Located directly across the street from the Biltmore Fashion Park shopping center in the heart of the Camelback Corridor business and shopping district, the Ritz-Carlton is the city's finest nonresort hotel, known for providing impeccable service. The public areas are filled with European antiques, and although this decor might seem a bit out of place in Phoenix, it's still utterly sophisticated. In the guest rooms, you'll find reproductions of antique furniture and marble bathrooms with ornate fixtures.

Dining/Diversions: Bistro 24 is a casual and lively French bistro. The elegant lobby lounge serves afternoon tea as well as cocktails, while in The Club, fine cigars and premium spirits are the order of the day.

Amenities: Small outdoor pool, fitness center, saunas, concierge, 24-hour room service, valet/laundry service, baby-sitting.

✪ **Royal Palms Hotel and Casitas.** 5200 E. Camelback Rd., Phoenix, AZ 85018. ☎ **800/672-6011** or 602/840-3610. Fax 602/840-6927. www.royalpalmshotel.com. 116 units. A/C TV TEL. Jan 1–early June $345–$495 double, $385–$3,500 suite; early June–early Sept $175–$295 double, $200–$2,500 suite; early Sept–Dec $295–$425 double, $335–$3,500 suite (all rates plus $16 daily service fee). AE, CB, DC, DISC, MC, V.

The Royal Palms, midway between Scottsdale and Biltmore Fashion Park, reopened in 1997 after a complete renovation and is now one of the finest, most romantic resorts in the valley. The main building, constructed more than 50 years ago, was built by Cunard Steamship executive Delos Cooke in the Spanish mission style and is filled with European antiques that once belonged to Cooke. Antique water fountains and lush walled gardens give the property the tranquil feel of a Mediterranean monastery cloister.

The most memorable rooms at the resort are the individually designed deluxe casitas. Each of these rooms has a distinctive decor (ranging from opulent contemporary to classic European). These rooms also have completely private back patios and front patios that can be enclosed by heavy curtains. Other rooms are luxuriously appointed, although not quite so opulent.

Dining/Diversions: T. Cook's serves Mediterranean cuisine amid European antiques and is one of the city's most romantic restaurants (see chapter 5). An adjacent bar/lounge conjures up a Spanish villa setting. There's also a poolside bar and grill.

Amenities: Swimming pool with cabanas, whirlpool, tennis court, large exercise room, concierge, 24-hour room service, valet/laundry service.

EXPENSIVE

Embassy Suites Biltmore. 2630 E. Camelback Rd., Phoenix, AZ 85016. ☎ **800/EMBASSY** or 602/955-3992. Fax 602/955-6479. 232 units. A/C TV TEL. Jan–Apr $239 double; May and Sept–Dec $179–$199 double; June–Aug $109–$119 double. Rates include full breakfast. AE, CB, DC, DISC, MC, V.

Located across the parking lot from the Biltmore Fashion Park (Phoenix's most upscale shopping center), this atrium hotel makes a great base if you want to be within walking distance of half a dozen good restaurants. The huge atrium is filled with interesting tile work and other artistic Southwestern touches, as well as tropical greenery, waterfalls, and ponds filled with koi (Japanese carp).

Unfortunately, the rooms, all suites, are dated and a bit of a let-down after passing through the atrium greenhouse, but they're certainly large. All have a microwave and refrigerator.

Dining/Diversions: The hotel's atrium houses the breakfast area and a romantic lounge with huge banquettes shaded by palm trees. Just off the atrium is a very contemporary high-end steakhouse. There's also a complimentary evening cocktail hour.

Amenities: Large outdoor pool, whirlpool, fitness room, concierge, room service, valet/laundry, courtesy car.

MODERATE

Hacienda Alta. 5750 E. Camelback Rd., Phoenix, AZ 85018. ☎ **480/945-8525.** 3 units. A/C TV. $100–$125 double; $150 suite. Rates include full breakfast. No credit cards.

Located adjacent to The Phoenician, yet very much in its own separate world surrounded by a desert landscape, this home offers a very convenient location, reasonable rates, and a chance to feel away from it all in the middle of the city. Don't expect the fussiness of most other B&Bs; owners Margaret and Ed Newhall make this casual, eclectic place a fun home away from home. The inn is housed in a 1920s territorial-style

Family-Friendly Hotels

Hyatt Regency Scottsdale *(see p. 42)* Not only is there a totally awesome water playground complete with sand beach and waterslide, but the Kamp Hyatt Kachina program provides supervised structured activities.

The Phoenician *(see p. 43)* Kids absolutely love the waterslide here, and kids and parents both appreciate the Funicians Club, a supervised activities program for children ages 5 to 12. A putting green and croquet court offer further diversions.

Doubletree La Posada Resort *(see p. 46)* If you're a kid, it's hard to imagine a cooler pool than the one here. It's got a two-story waterfall, a swim-through cave, and big artificial boulders. There are also horseshoe pits, a volleyball court, and a pitch-and-putt green.

Pointe Hilton Squaw Peak Resort *(see p. 59)* A waterslide, a tubing river, a waterfall, water volleyball, a miniature golf course, a video games room, and a kids' program guarantee that your kids will be exhausted by the end of the day.

Holiday Inn SunSpree Resort *(see p. 49)* Economical rates, a good Scottsdale location adjacent to the McCormick-Stillman Railroad Park, lots of grass for running around on, and free meals for kids under 12 make this one of the valley's best choice for families on a budget.

adobe home, and in the old gardens you'll find orange and grapefruit trees, which often provide juice for breakfast. There's also a large suite with a sleeping loft, whirlpool tub, fireplace, and balcony overlooking the Phoenician's golf course.

Maricopa Manor. 15 W. Pasadena Ave., Phoenix, AZ 85013. ☎ **800/292-6403** or 602/274-6302. Fax 602/266-3904. www.maricopamanor.com. 6 suites. A/C TV TEL. Sept–May $149–$229 double; June–Aug $89–$129 double. Rates include continental breakfast. AE, DC, DISC, MC, V.

Centrally located between downtown Phoenix and Scottsdale, this B&B is just a block off busy Camelback Road and for many years has been one of Phoenix's only official B&Bs. The inn's main home, designed to resemble a Spanish manor house, was built in 1928 and the many orange trees, palms, and large yard all lend a country air. All the guest rooms are large suites, and although the furnishings seem a bit dated, the rooms are quite comfortable. One suite has a sunroom and kitchen, and another has two separate sleeping areas. There are tables in the garden where you can eat your breakfast, which is delivered to your door. The inn also has a pool and hot tub.

Sierra Suites. 5235 N. 16th St., Phoenix, AZ 85016. ☎ **800/4-SIERRA** or 602/265-6800. Fax 602/265-1114. 113 units. A/C TV TEL. Oct–Apr $119–$139; May–Sept $49–$59. AE, DISC, MC, V.

Billing itself as a temporary residence and offering discounts for stays of 5 days or more, this hotel consists of studio-style apartments and is located just north of Camelback Road and not far from Biltmore Fashion Park. Although designed primarily for corporate business travelers on temporary assignment in the area, this hotel makes a good choice for families as well. All rooms have full kitchens, big closets and bathrooms, and separate sitting areas. Facilities include an exercise room, a pool, and a whirlpool. Local phone calls are free.

4 North Phoenix

VERY EXPENSIVE

✪ **Pointe Hilton Squaw Peak Resort.** 7677 N. 16th St., Phoenix, AZ 85020-9832. ☎ **800/876-4683** or 602/997-2626. Fax 602/997-2391. www.pointehilton.com. 564 units. A/C MINIBAR TV TEL. Jan–late Apr $239–$329 double, $839 grande suite; late Apr–late May and early Sept–Dec $189–$249 double, $729 grande suite; late May–early Sept $99–$149 double, $449 grande suite (all rates plus $8 daily resort fee). AE, CB, DC, DISC, EC, JCB, MC, V.

Located at the foot of Squaw Peak, this lushly landscaped resort in north Phoenix makes a big splash with its Hole-in-the-Wall River Ranch, a 9-acre aquatic playground that features a tubing "river," waterslide, waterfall, sports pool, and lagoon pool. An 18-hole putting course, game room, and children's activity center also help make it a great family vacation spot. The resort is done in the Spanish villa style, and most of the guest rooms are large, two-room suites outfitted with a mix of contemporary and Spanish colonial–style furnishings.

Dining/Diversions: The resort has a Mexican restaurant in an 1880 adobe building plus a Western-theme restaurant. There's also a more upscale dining room that serves contemporary American and Southwestern dishes.

Amenities: In addition to the River Ranch pools, there are four other pools, several whirlpools, a full-service spa (with racquetball courts, fitness room, lap pool, sauna, steam room, and aerobics classes), an 18-hole golf course (4 miles away), four tennis courts, jogging trails, rental bikes, shops, business center, concierge, room service, valet/laundry service, rental-car desk, baby-sitting, and children's programs.

Pointe Hilton Tapatio Cliffs Resort. 11111 N. Seventh St., Phoenix, AZ 85020. ☎ **800/876-4683** or 602/866-7500. Fax 602/993-0276. www.pointhilton.com. 585 units. A/C MINIBAR TV TEL. Jan–late Apr $239–$329 double, $909 grande suite; late Apr–late May and early Sept–Dec $189–$249 double, $739 grande suite; late May–early Sept $99–$149 double, $549 grande suite (all rates plus $8 daily resort fee). AE, CB, DC, DISC, EC, JCB, MC, V.

If you love to lounge by the pool, then this resort is a great choice. The Falls, a 3-acre water playground, includes two lagoon pools, a 138-foot waterslide, 40-foot-high cascades, a whirlpool tucked into an artificial grotto, and poolside rental cabanas for that extra dash of luxury. Hikers will enjoy the easy access to trails in the adjacent North Mountain Recreation Area, while golfers can avail themselves of the resort's golf course. There's also a small full-service health spa. All rooms are spacious suites with Southwest furnishings, and the corner rooms, with their extra windows, are particularly bright. Situated on the shoulder of North Mountain, Tapatio Cliffs offers the steepest grounds of Phoenix's three Pointe resorts (get your heart and brakes checked).

Dining/Diversions: Different Pointe of View offers stupendous hilltop views, an expensive international menu, and an extensive wine cellar (see chapter 5). There's also a casual steakhouse and a more formal, club-like dining room. There are two poolside cafes.

Amenities: In addition to facilities mentioned above, there are 12 tennis courts, five other pools, whirlpools, a fitness center with steam room and sauna, rental bikes, a golf and tennis shop, a business center, a concierge, room service, rental-car desk, free shuttle between Pointe Hilton properties, horseback riding, and baby-sitting.

Sheraton Crescent Hotel. 2620 W. Dunlap Ave., Phoenix, AZ 85021. ☎ **800/423-4126** or 602/943-8200. Fax 602/371-2856. www.arizonaguide.com/sheratoncrescent. 342 units. A/C TV TEL. Jan to mid-Apr $250–$280 double, from $400 suite; mid-Apr to late May and mid-Sept to Dec $130–$230, from $230 suite; late May to mid-Sept $59–$135 double, from $230 suite. AE, CB, DC, DISC, MC, V. Small pets accepted.

Located in Phoenix's north-central business district and across I-17 from the Metrocenter mall, this business hotel is a sister property to The Phoenician and displays much the same decorative style (with lots of marble), albeit on a more subdued level. Although situated away from downtown and the Camelback Corridor business districts, this is still one of the city's better choices for business travelers, especially if you appreciate an abundance of athletic facilities. Guest rooms are designed with business travelers in mind, and provide plenty of space, comfort, and convenience. The king rooms with balconies are worth asking for.

Dining/Diversions: The hotel's big, casual restaurant serves new American cuisine. There's also a small lounge.

Amenities: The hotel's small main pool is in a lush garden setting and has a long waterslide that's a hit with kids. Other facilities include a large fitness center, whirlpool, sauna, two tennis courts, two squash courts, and volleyball and basketball courts. Concierge, room service, and valet/laundry service are available.

EXPENSIVE

Embassy Suites—Phoenix North. 2577 W. Greenway Rd., Phoenix, AZ 85023-4222. ☎ **800/EMBASSY** or 602/375-1777. Fax 602/375-4012. www.embassy-suites.com. 314 units. A/C TV TEL. Nov–Apr $129–$159 double; May–Oct $89–$109 double. Rates include full breakfast. AE, CB, DC, DISC, MC, V.

This resort-like hotel in north Phoenix is right off I-17 and well away from the rest of the valley's resorts (and good restaurants), but if you happen to have relatives in Sun City or are planning a trip north to Sedona, it's a good choice. The lobby of the Mission-style, all-suite hotel has the feel of a Spanish church interior, but instead of a cloister off the lobby, there is a garden courtyard with a huge swimming pool and lots of palm trees. The guest rooms are all suites, although furnishings are fairly basic, and bathrooms are small.

Dining/Diversions: The casual restaurant in the lobby serves moderately priced meals. There's also a piano lounge and poolside bar. Complimentary evening cocktails.

Amenities: Large pool, two tennis courts, exercise room, whirlpool, sauna, sand volleyball court, two racquetball courts, room service, valet/laundry service.

MODERATE/INEXPENSIVE

Among the better moderately priced chain motels in north Phoenix are the **Best Western InnSuites Hotel Phoenix,** 1615 E. Northern Ave. at 16th Street (☎ **602/997-6285**), charging $99 to $129 double; and the **Best Western Bell Motel,** 17211 N. Black Canyon Hwy. (☎ **602/993-8300**), charging $89 to $109 double. Rates are for the high season; for toll-free phone numbers.

Among the better budget chain motels in the north Phoenix area are the **Motel 6—Sweetwater,** 2735 W. Sweetwater Ave. (☎ **602/942-5030**), charging $50 to $56 double; and **Super 8—Phoenix Metro/Central,** 4021 N. 27th Ave. (☎ **602/248-8880**), charging $50 to $56 double. Rates are for the high season.

5 Downtown Phoenix

VERY EXPENSIVE

Crowne Plaza—Phoenix Downtown. 100 N. First St., Phoenix, AZ 85004. ☎ **800/2CROWNE** or 602/333-0000. Fax 602/333-5181. 532 units. A/C TV TEL. Oct–Apr $239–$279 double; June–Sept $139–$179 double. AE, DC, DISC, JCB, MC, V. Valet parking $10.

This 19-story business and convention hotel is your best choice in downtown, although with the crowds of conventioneers, individual travelers are likely to feel overlooked. A Mediterranean villa theme has been adopted throughout the public areas with slate flooring and walls painted to resemble cracked stucco. Guest rooms continue the Mediterranean feel and are designed with the business traveler in mind.

Dining/Diversions: There's a cafe for breakfast and a bar and grill with a bit of character (but very standard fare).

Amenities: Fitness room, swimming pool, whirlpool spa, room service, concierge, massages, valet/laundry service, business center.

EXPENSIVE

Hyatt Regency Phoenix. 122 N. 2nd St., Phoenix, AZ 85004. ☎ **800/233-1234** or 602/252-1234. Fax 602/254-9472. www.phoenix.hyatt.com. 712 units. A/C TV TEL. $134–$274 double; $450–$1,550 suite. AE, CB, DC, DISC, JCB, MC, V. Valet parking $17; self-parking $12.

Located directly across the street from the Phoenix Civic Plaza, this high-rise Hyatt is almost always packed with conventioneers. Whether full or empty, the hotel always seems somewhat understaffed, so don't expect top-notch service if you're stuck here on a convention. However, the attractive lobby certainly provides plenty of space for lounging. The rooms are fairly standard, although comfortably furnished. Ask for a room above the eighth floor to take advantage of the views from the glass elevators.

Dining/Diversions: The Compass Room is Arizona's only rotating rooftop restaurant and serves Southwestern dishes. The food is usually decent, and the views are interesting. There's also the more casual and inexpensive Terrace Café in the hotel's atrium and a contemporary restaurant/bar at street level.

Amenities: Small outdoor pool, exercise room, whirlpool, tennis courts, shopping arcade, concierge, room service, valet/laundry service.

MODERATE

✪ **Hotel San Carlos.** 202 N. Central Ave., Phoenix, AZ 85004. ☎ **602/253-4121.** Fax 602/253-6668. www.hotelsancarlos.com. 132 units. A/C TV TEL. Jan–Apr $139 double, $185 suite; May–Sept $89 double, $125 suite; Oct–Dec $105 double, $169 suite. Rates include continental breakfast. AE, CB, DC, DISC, MC, V. Valet and self-parking $15. Pets allowed, $25.

If you don't mind staying in downtown Phoenix with the convention crowds, you'll get a good value at this historic hotel. Built in 1928 and listed on the National Register of Historic Places, the San Carlos is a small hotel that provides that touch of elegance and charm missing from the other downtown hotels. Unfortunately, rooms are rather small by today's standards and the decor needs updating. There's an Italian restaurant in the lobby, an adjacent espresso bar, and an Irish pub. The hotel also features valet/laundry service and a rooftop pool.

6 Tempe, Mesa, South Phoenix & the Airport Area

VERY EXPENSIVE

The Pointe Hilton South Mountain Resort. 7777 S. Pointe Pkwy., Phoenix, AZ 85044. ☎ **800/876-4683** or 602/438-9000. Fax 602/431-6535. www.pointehilton.com. 638 units. A/C MINIBAR TV TEL. Jan–late Apr $239–$329 double, $869 grande suite; late Apr–late May and early Sept–Dec $189–$249 double, $729 grande suite; late May–early Sept $99–$149 double, $539 grande suite (all rates plus $8 daily resort fee). AE, CB, DC, DISC, EC, JCB, MC, V.

On the south side of the valley, this Pointe Hilton resort abuts the 17,000-acre South Mountain Park, and although the grand scale of the resort seems designed primarily to accommodate convention crowds, individual travelers, especially active ones, will find plenty to keep them busy here. Golfers get great views from the greens, urban cowboys can ride right into the sunset on South Mountain, and if it's abs and pecs you want to work on, the 40,000-square-foot fitness center should keep you pumped up.

The guest rooms here are all suites and feature contemporary Southwestern furnishings. Mountainside suites offer the best views of the golf course and South Mountain.

Dining/Diversions: Rustler's Rooste is a Western-themed restaurant featuring cowboy bands and rattlesnake appetizers (see chapter 5). A second restaurant features continental cuisine and a more sedate atmosphere. There's also a casual Mexican restaurant and a place for healthful meals at the fitness center.

Amenities: Two 18-hole golf courses, 10 tennis courts, four racquetball courts, six swimming pools, volleyball courts, riding stables, pro shop, health club, concierge, room service, valet/laundry service, massages, rental-car desk, baby-sitting.

✪ **Wyndham Buttes Resort.** 2000 Westcourt Way, Tempe, AZ 85282. ☎ **800/WYNDHAM** or 602/225-9000. Fax 602/438-8622. www.wyndham.com. 353 units. A/C MINIBAR TV TEL. Labor Day–late May $215–$294 double, from $475 suite; late May–Labor Day $99–$159 double, from $375 suite. AE, CB, DC, DISC, MC, V.

This spectacular resort, only 3 miles from Sky Harbor Airport, makes the utmost of its craggy hilltop location (although some people complain that the freeway in the foreground ruins the view). Few other valley resorts have as much of a sense of place; the rocky setting and desert landscaping leave no doubt you're in the Southwest. From the cactus garden, stream, and waterfall in the lobby to the circular restaurant and the freeform swimming pools, every inch of this resort is calculated to take your breath away. The pools (complete with waterfalls) and four whirlpools (one is the most romantic in the valley) are the best reasons to stay here.

Guest rooms are stylishly elegant, and many have views across the valley (marred slightly by the adjacent freeway). The highway-view rooms are a bit larger than the pool-view rooms, but second floor pool-view rooms have patios.

Unfortunately for fans of long soaks, most bathrooms have only ¾-size tubs (but there are great whirlpool spas around the grounds).

Dining/Diversions: The Top of the Rock restaurant snags the best view around, and sunset dinners are memorable (see chapter 5). An informal dining room, complete with waterfall and fishpond, is located below the lobby. There are bars below Top of the Rock (with only a partial view), in the lobby, and by the pool.

Amenities: Four tennis courts, a fitness center, concierge, room service, valet/laundry service, a business center.

EXPENSIVE

✪ **Fiesta Inn.** 2100 S. Priest Dr., Tempe, AZ 85282. ☎ **800/528-6481** or 480/967-1441. Fax 480/967-0224. 270 units. A/C TV TEL. Jan 1–late Apr $155 double; late Apr–May $119 double; June–Sept $85 double; Oct–Dec $139 double. AE, CB, DC, DISC, MC, V. Pets accepted.

Reasonable rates, shady grounds, extensive recreational facilities (three tennis courts, putting green, driving range, pool, and fitness room), and a location close to the airport, ASU, and Tempe's Mill Avenue make this older, casual resort one of the best deals in the valley. Okay, so it isn't as fancy as the resorts in Scottsdale, but you can't argue with the rates. Guest rooms are large, with refrigerators, coffeemakers, and hair dryers, and local phone calls are free.

Dining/Diversions: The restaurant serves reliable American fare, and there's also a lounge.

Amenities: Room service, concierge, complimentary airport shuttle, valet/laundry service.

Tempe Mission Palms Hotel. 60 E. 5th St., Tempe, AZ 85281. ☎ **800/547-8705** or 480/894-1400. Fax 480/968-7677. www.missionpalms.com. 303 units. A/C TV TEL. Jan–May $179–$279 double, $229–$299 suite; June–Aug $99–$159 double, $129–$179 suite; Sept–Dec $169–$239 double, $199–$259 suite. AE, CB, DC, DISC, JCB, MC, V.

College students, their families, and anyone else who wants to be close to Tempe's nightlife will find this an ideal, although somewhat overpriced, location right in the heart of the Mill Avenue shopping, restaurant, and nightlife district. When you've had enough of the hustle and bustle on Mill Avenue, you can retreat to the hotel's rooftop pool. For the most part, guest rooms are quite comfortable and boast lots of wood, marble, and granite.

Dining/Diversions: The hotel's restaurant serves Southwestern meals at reasonable prices. You'll also find a lounge off the lobby and a poolside bar.

Amenities: Medium-size outdoor pool, tennis court, fitness center, whirlpool, sauna, business center, room service, complimentary airport shuttle, valet/laundry service.

Twin Palms Hotel. 225 E. Apache Blvd., Tempe, AZ 85281. ☎ **800/367-0835** or 480/967-9431. Fax 480/968-1877. 140 units. A/C TV TEL. Jan–Apr $159 double; May–Sept $79 double; Oct–Dec $129 double. $170–$350 suite year-round. AE, CB, DC, DISC, MC, V.

Although the rooms at this midrise hotel just off the ASU campus are just standard rooms (with coffeemakers), the Twin Palms is a great choice for fitness fanatics. Hotel guests have full access to the nearby ASU Student Recreation Complex, which covers 135,000 square feet and includes a huge weight-training room; Olympic pool; and racquetball, tennis, and basketball courts. When you stay here, you're also close to Sun Devil Stadium, the ASU-Karsten Golf Course, and busy Mill Avenue.

Diversions: There's a small bar off the lobby.

Amenities: In addition to fitness center access, there's a complimentary airport shuttle, and local phone calls are free.

MODERATE/INEXPENSIVE

Apache Boulevard in Tempe becomes Main Street in Mesa, and along this stretch of road there are numerous old motels charging some of the lowest rates in the valley. However, these motels are very hit-or-miss. If you're used to staying at nonchain motels, you might want to cruise this strip and check out a few places. Otherwise, try the chain motels mentioned below (which tend to charge $20 to $40 more per night than nonchain motels).

Chain motel options in the Tempe area include the **Days Inn—Tempe,** 1221 E. Apache Blvd. (☎ **480/968-7793**), charging $69 to $124 double; **Super 8—Tempe/Scottsdale,** 1020 E. Apache Blvd. (☎ **480/967-8891**), charging $67 to $81 double; and **Travelodge—Tempe,** 1005 E. Apache Blvd. (☎ **480/968-7871**), charging $59 to $99 double.

Chain motel options in the Mesa area include the **Days Inn—Mesa,** 333 W. Juanita Ave. (☎ **480/844-8900**), charging $86 to $106 double; **Motel 6—Mesa North,** 336 W.

Hampton Ave. (☎ **480/844-8899**), charging $54 double; and **Super 8—Mesa,** 6733 E. Main St. (☎ **480/981-6181**), charging $67 to $69 double.

Chain motels in the airport area include the **Best Western Airport Inn,** 2425 S. 24th St. (☎ **602/273-7251**), charging $90 to $120 double, and **Rodeway Inn Airport East,** 1550 S. 52nd St. (☎ **480/967-3000**), charging $80 to $110 double. Rates are for the high season.

7 Outlying Resorts

Gold Canyon Golf Resort. 6100 S. Kings Ranch Rd., Gold Canyon, AZ 85219. ☎ **800/624-6445** or 480/982-9090. Fax 480/983-9554. www.gcgr.com. 101 units. A/C TV TEL. Mid-Jan to mid-Apr $200–$230 double; mid-Apr to Sept $125–$155 double; Oct to mid-Jan $175–$205 double. AE, DC, DISC, MC, V.

Located way out on the east side of the valley near Apache Junction, Gold Canyon is a favorite of devoted golfers who come to play some of the most scenic holes in the state (the Superstition Mountains provide the backdrop). Although nongolfers will appreciate the scenery here, the small pool makes it clear that golfers, not swimmers, take the fore here. The guest rooms, housed in blindingly white pueblo-inspired buildings, are large, and some have fireplaces while others have whirlpools.

Dining/Diversions: The main dining room serves Southwestern and new American fare, and there's a bar and grill serving simple meals.

Amenities: Two gorgeous 18-hole golf courses, two tennis courts, a pool, a whirlpool, horseback riding, rental bikes, room service.

The Wigwam Resort. 300 Wigwam Blvd., Litchfield Park, AZ 85340. ☎ **800/327-0396** or 623/935-3811. Fax 623/935-3737. www.wigwamresort.com. 331 units. A/C MINIBAR TV TEL. Early Jan–early May $330–$390 double, $390–$525 suite; early May–late June $245–$295 double, $295–$380 suite; late June–early Sept $145–$185 double, $185–$275 suite; early Sept–early Jan $245–$295 double, $295–$430 suite. AE, CB, DC, DISC, MC, V. Pets under 20 lbs. accepted ($50 deposit, $25 nonrefundable).

Located 20 minutes west of downtown Phoenix and twice as far from Scottsdale, this resort opened its doors to the public in 1929 and remains one of the nation's premier golf resorts. Three challenging golf courses and superb service are the reasons most people choose this resort, which, although elegant, is set amid flat lands that lack the stunning desert scenery of the Scottsdale area.

Most of the guest rooms are in Santa Fe–style buildings, surrounded by green lawns and colorful gardens. All rooms are spacious and feature contemporary Southwestern furniture. Some rooms have fireplaces, but the most popular rooms are those along the golf course.

Dining/Diversions: The resort's Terrace Dining Room serves continental cuisine, and the Arizona Kitchen serves acclaimed Southwestern fare. There's also a clubhouse restaurant and a poolside bar and grill. Afternoon tea and evening cocktails are served in a lobby lounge, and there's also a sports bar.

Amenities: Three golf courses, putting green, golf lessons, nine tennis courts, tennis lessons, pro shop, two pools, bicycles, volleyball, croquet, trap and skeet shooting, exercise room, sauna, holiday and summer children's programs, concierge, room service, valet/laundry service, massages.

5

Dining

Just as the Valley of the Sun boasts some terrific resorts, it is also full of excellent restaurants, and Scottsdale and the Biltmore Corridor are home to most of the city's best dining establishments. If you have only one expensive meal while you're here, I'd suggest a resort restaurant that offers a view of the city lights. Other meals not to be missed are the cowboy dinners served amid Wild West decor at such places as Pinnacle Peak and Rustler's Rooste.

Phoenix also has plenty of those big and familiar chains that you've heard so much about. There's a **Hard Rock Cafe,** 2621 E. Camelback Rd. (☎ **602/956-3669**) where you can toss down a burger and then buy that all-important T-shirt to prove you've been here. As Phoenix has become more and more Arizona's version of Los Angeles, it has also acquired all the important California chains, such as **California Pizza Kitchen,** 2400 E. Camelback Rd. (☎ **602/553-8382**), located in Biltmore Fashion Park, and also in Scottsdale at 10100 Scottsdale Rd. at Gold Dust Avenue (☎ **480/596-8300**).

The big chain steakhouses are also duking it out here in Phoenix. You'll find two **Ruth's Chris** steakhouses: in the Biltmore district at 2201 E. Camelback Rd. (☎ **602/957-9600**) and in the Scottsdale Seville shopping plaza, 7001 N. Scottsdale Rd., Scottsdale (☎ **480/991-5988**). You'll find **Morton's Steakhouses** in the Biltmore district at 2501 E. Camelback Rd. (☎ **602/955-9577**) and in north Scottsdale across from the Scottsdale airport, 15233 N. Kierland Blvd. (☎ **480/951-4440**).

Good places to go trolling for a place to eat include the trendy Biltmore Fashion Park and Old Town Scottsdale. At the former, which by the way is a shopping mall, not a park, you'll find the above mentioned chain restaurant—California Pizza Kitchen—as well as nearly a dozen other excellent restaurants. In Old Town Scottsdale, within an area of

Phoenix, Scottsdale & the Valley of the Sun Dining

0
3 mi
0
3 km
N
under construction
Bell Rd.
Greenway Rd.
Thunderbird Rd.
Sweetwater Ave.
Cactus Rd.
Shea Blvd.
Frank Lloyd Wright Blvd.
Doubletree Ranch Rd.
Dreamy Draw Recreation Area
Paradise Valley
Squaw Peak Recreation Area
Indian Bend Rd.
Lincoln Dr.
McDonald Dr.
Camelback Mountain Recreation Area
To Payson
Camelback Rd.
Indian School Rd.
Beeline Hwy.
Osborn Rd.
Thomas Rd.
Scottsdale
McDowell Rd.
Papago Park
Van Buren St.
McKellips Rd.
Mesa
Sky Harbor International Airport
Salt River
University Dr.
Tempe
Apache Blvd.
Main St.
Broadway Rd.
Hohokam Expy.
Southern Ave.
Superstition Freeway
Baseline Rd.
Guadalupe Rd.
Elliot Rd.
Warner Rd.
Ray Rd.
Chandler Blvd.
Williams Field Rd.
Pecos Rd.
To Tucson
Squaw Peak Pkwy.
Cave Creek Rd.
32nd St.
Tatum Rd.
56th St.
Invergordon Rd.
Scottsdale Rd.
Hayden Rd.
Pima Rd.
96th St.
104th St.
40th St.
44th St.
48th St.
52nd St.
64th St.
68th St.
Miller Rd.
Dobson Rd.
Country Club Dr.
Mesa Dr.
Stapley Dr.
24th St.
Priest Dr.
Mill Ave.
Rural Rd.
McClintock Dr.
Price Rd.
Alma School Rd.
Arizona Ave.
McQueen Rd.
Cooper Rd.
Gilbert Rd.

roughly 4 square blocks, you'll find about a dozen good restaurants. A few of our favorites in both places are listed here.

Phoenix is a sprawling city, and it can be a real pain to have to drive around in search of a good lunch spot. If you happen to be visiting the Phoenix Art Museum, the Heard Museum, or the Desert Botanical Gardens anytime around lunch, stay put for your noon meal. All three of these attractions have cafes serving decent, if limited, menus.

1 Scottsdale

EXPENSIVE

The Chaparral. At Marriott's Camelback Inn, 5402 E. Lincoln Dr. ☎ **480/948-1700,** ext. 7888. Reservations highly recommended. Main courses $22–$34. AE, CB, DC, DISC, MC, V. Daily 6–10pm. NEW AMERICAN.

They've changed the decor and the menu, but rest assured that Camelback Mountain is still the view out the window. No longer does the menu feature the timeless continental classics it once did. These days you'll start off with herb-laced focaccia, potato rolls, and salted rosemary lavosh—all incredibly tempting. The rich lobster bisque—covered with puff pastry and served with a spoonful of caviar crème fraîche—is a holdover from the old menu; it's an elegant dining experience not to be missed. Some dishes are more successful than others. Hits include a moist and flavorful sea bass crusted with tomato and parsley, and, for garlic lovers, lobster tail with aïoli (garlic mayonnaise). Service is as attentive as you would expect, and some wines are even fairly moderately priced. It's not as formal an environment as it once was—you can now get away with dressing "comfortably casual" here.

El Chorro Lodge. 5550 E. Lincoln Dr. ☎ **480/948-5170.** Reservations recommended. Lunch $8–$17; full dinner $12–$63. AE, CB, DC, DISC, MC, V. Mon–Fri 11am–3pm and 5:30–11pm; Sat–Sun 5:30–11pm. CONTINENTAL.

Built in 1934 as a school for girls and converted to a lodge and restaurant 3 years later, El Chorro Lodge is a valley landmark set on its own 22 acres of desert. It's one of the area's last old traditional restaurants. At night, lights twinkle on the saguaro cactus, and the restaurant takes on a timeless tranquility, even if the interior is a little dowdy. The adobe building houses several dining rooms, but the patio is the place to sit, either in the daytime or on a chilly night near the crackling fireplace. The traditional decor and menu that features such classic dishes as chateaubriand and rack of lamb are popular with both old-timers and families. In addition to the favorites, there are several dishes low in salt and fat, as well as seafood dishes. Save room for the legendary sticky buns.

Golden Swan. At the Hyatt Regency Scottsdale Resort, 7500 E. Doubletree Ranch Rd. ☎ **480/991-3388.** Reservations recommended. Main courses $27.50–$36; Sun brunch $34. AE, DC, DISC, MC, V. Daily 6–10pm; Sun brunch 9:30am–2pm. REGIONAL AMERICAN.

At this restaurant within the Hyatt Regency Scottsdale Resort, a combination of cuisine and setting make for very special meals. Dramatically spotlit royal palms, geometric architecture, and the sound of fountains and waterfalls set the tone; the food is just as pleasurable, beautifully presented with plenty of attention to details. Artistically arranged entrees generally offer several distinctive flavors, some subtle, some bold—for example, orange-honey barbecued salmon on a truffle oil–risotto cake or a grilled lamb chop with jalapeño-honey mustard crusted with toasted pistachios and served with a cheddar cheese hominy timbale. Save room for one of the Golden Swan's decadent desserts—perhaps a silky chocolate mousse cake with fresh berries soaked in zinfandel sauce accented by bright green crushed pistachios. Before or after dinner, the open-air lounge at the resort is a romantic place to have a drink and listen to live music.

Mancuso's. At the Borgata, 6166 N. Scottsdale Rd. ☎ **480/948-9988.** Reservations recommended. Main courses $18–$29; pastas $17–$24. AE, CB, DC, DISC, MC, V. Daily 5–10:30pm. NORTHERN ITALIAN/CONTINENTAL.

With its ramparts, towers, stone walls, and narrow, uneven alleyways leading through the complex, the Borgata is built in the style of a medieval Italian village, so it seems only fitting that Mancuso's would affect the look of an elaborate baronial banquet hall. A cathedral ceiling, arched windows, and huge roof beams set the stage for the gourmet continental cuisine; and a pianist playing soft jazz sets the mood. If you lack the means to start your meal with the beluga caviar, perhaps *carpaccio di manzo*—sliced raw beef with mustard sauce and capers—will do. Veal is a specialty, but it is always difficult just to get past the pasta offerings. Lately, more fish and daily seafood specials have been added to the menu. The professional service will have you feeling like royalty by the time you finish your dessert and coffee.

✪ **Mary Elaine's.** At The Phoenician, 6000 E. Camelback Rd., Scottsdale. ☎ **480/423-2530.** Reservations highly recommended. Jacket required for men. Main courses $37–$45; 6-course seasonal tasting menu $110 (matched wines are an additional $55). AE, CB, DC, DISC, MC, V. Mon–Thurs 6–10pm; Fri–Sat 6–11pm. FRENCH/MEDITERRANEAN.

Located on the top floor of The Phoenician's main building, Mary Elaine's is one of the finest restaurants in the valley and boasts one of the best views as well. The restaurant is the height of elegance and sophistication (Austrian crystal, French Ercuis silver, and Wedgwood china), although those seeking a more casual, alfresco setting can dine on the patio most of the year.

The chef focuses on the flavors of the modern French kitchen, which are usually dictated by the changing seasons. A recent menu included seared foie gras with 100-year-old balsamic vinegar, John Dory fish with fennel, artichokes, and pearl onions, and red currant–glazed rack of venison. Mary Elaine's will go out of its way to accommodate a vegetarian—call beforehand to make a request. The very extensive wine list has won numerous awards.

Windows on the Green. At The Phoenician, 6000 E. Camelback Rd., Scottsdale. ☎ **480/423-2530.** Reservations recommended. Main courses $18.50–$42; regional tasting menu $59. AE, CB, DC, DISC, MC, V. Wed–Mon 6–10pm. SOUTHWESTERN.

Slightly more casual than The Phoenician's premier restaurant, Mary Elaine's, but no less elegant, Windows on the Green has a sweeping view of the resort's golf course. Chef Michael Snoke turns the familiar into the extraordinary when serving up such dishes as quail stuffed with jalapeño cheddar grits, blue cornmeal–crusted trout, and prickly pear sorbet. While the flavors on the menu here are predominantly Southwestern, not every dish is doused with chili peppers. Diners with sensitive palates will find plenty to choose from. The wine list is chosen to complement these regional flavors. All in all, a good but somewhat pricey introduction to Southwestern cuisine.

MODERATE

Another area restaurant worth trying is **Sam's Cafe,** North Scottsdale Road and Shea Boulevard (☎ **480/368-2800**), which has other branches around the valley. For more information on Sam's Cafe, see "Downtown Phoenix," later in this chapter.

✪ **Café Terra Cotta.** At the Borgata, 6166 N. Scottsdale Rd., Suite 100. ☎ **480/948-8100.** Reservations recommended for dinner. Main courses $8–$22. AE, DC, DISC, MC, V. Daily 11:30am–9:30pm. SOUTHWESTERN.

Café Terra Cotta started out in Tucson, where it invented the concept of trendy foods, and they haven't stopped cookin' since. The list of Southwestern choices at this casually sophisticated and low-key restaurant is long, including wood-oven pizzas, sandwiches, and smaller meals as well as full-size main courses. Imaginative combinations are the rule, so you'll want to take your time with the menu before ordering. For example, roll this over your imaginary taste buds: chili-roasted duck breast with chipotle sauce on a potato-horseradish pancake and carrot-jicama salad. Don't miss the garlic custard with warm salsa vinaigrette, which goes great with a glass of wine chosen from the well-rounded wine list.

Cowboy Ciao Wine Bar & Grill. 7133 E. Stetson Dr. (corner 6th Ave.). ☎ **480/WINE-111.** Reservations recommended. Main courses $7–$11 at lunch, $12–$24 at dinner. AE, DC, DISC, MC, V. Tues–Sat 11:30am–2pm and 5–10pm; Sun 5–10pm. SOUTHWESTERN/ITALIAN.

Delicious food, low prices, and a fun and trendy atmosphere furnished in "cowboy chic"—that sums up what makes Cowboy Ciao a great place for a meal. Located in fashionable downtown Scottsdale, this place attracts a diverse group of people who like to dive into the likes of cocoa-dusted scallops with peanut sauce or grilled halibut with a lemon-pepper couscous. Large, fresh salads get two thumbs up. Cowboy Ciao is also notable for its wine list and bar, where customers can order a flight (tasting assortment) of wines. We wouldn't miss the chocolate lottery dessert, consisting of a double chocolate and espresso torte plus an Arizona state lottery ticket.

✪ **Franco's Trattoria.** 8120 N. Hayden Rd. ☎ **480/948-6655.** Reservations recommended. Main courses $7–$11 at lunch, $12.50–$26 at dinner. AE, MC, V. Tues–Fri 11:30am–2pm and 5:15–10pm; Sat 5:15–10pm. Open Mon for both lunch and dinner Oct–Mar. Closed July. TUSCAN ITALIAN.

Dining at Franco's Trattoria is like taking a trip to Tuscany. Franco bustles around shaving hard cheeses, which arrive on the table accompanied by bread and olive oil, and chats with his regulars in an atmosphere that's both congenial and romantic. For starters, the *insalata capricciosa,* a salad of fennel, goat cheese, sun-dried tomatoes, beans, arugula, radicchio, and red onion, fairly bursts with flavor, as do the homemade raviolis and risottos. If you want something spicy (you are in the Southwest), try the *spezzatino di vitello dolce forte,* veal with tomato, rosemary, raisins, vinegar, and hot pepper. Lots of places claim to make the world's best tiramisu, but Franco's, made from his grandmother's recipe, truly takes the cake. It's the best you'll ever have, and it packs a wallop with its brandy, amaretto, and espresso-infused ladyfingers. Wines are very reasonably priced, and the service is knowledgeable and personable.

L'Ecole. At the Scottsdale Culinary Institute, 8100 E. Camelback Rd. (just east of Hayden Rd.). ☎ **480/990-7639.** Reservations highly recommended several days in advance. 3 courses $9.25–$13 at lunch, 5 courses $25 at dinner. DISC, MC, V. Mon–Fri 11:30am–1pm and 6–7:30pm. Closed every 3rd Monday. CONTINENTAL/INTERNATIONAL.

This culinary opportunity is a well-kept local secret—there aren't many places where you can get a three-course lunch for under $10 or a five-course dinner for $25. In spite of the fact that you don't have to bring a lot of money here, you do have to have a lot of patience—the cooking and serving is done by students, and it's all a learning experience for them. For an appetizer, you might try the wild raspberry salad; for an entree, sole français is nice, followed by crème brûlée or pecan pie. There is a respectable selection of wines and liquors to accompany the meal. This is such a good deal that people drive from all over the valley to eat here.

Pepin. 7363 Scottsdale Mall. ☎ **480/990-9026.** Reservations recommended. Main courses $13–$25; tapas $5–$9. AE, CB, DC, DISC, MC, V. Tues–Thurs 11:30am–3pm and 4:30–10pm; Fri–Sat 11:30am–3pm and 4:30–11pm; Sun 5–10pm. Happy hour, Tues–Fri 4:30–6:30pm. SPANISH.

For traditional Spanish fare and plenty of lively entetainment, you won't do better than Pepin. Located on the Scottsdale Mall, this small Spanish restaurant offers such a wide selection of tapas that you can easily have dinner without ever glancing at the main-course list. However, there are also several styles of paella, most of which are seafood extrava-ganzas. Thursday through Saturday evenings, there are live flamenco performances, and Friday and Saturday evenings, there's also salsa dancing. Call for times.

Rancho Pinot. 6208 N. Scottsdale Rd. (south of Lincoln Dr.). ☎ **602/468-9463.** Reservations recommended. Main courses $17–$26. AE, DISC, MC, V. Tues–Sat 5:30–10pm. Summer hours subject to change. CONTEMPORARY AMERICAN.

Rancho Pinot, in a shopping center adjacent to the Borgata, combines a "homey" cowboy chic decor with nonthreatening contemporary American cuisine and has long been a favorite with Scottsdale and Phoenix residents. The menu here changes regularly and tends to emphasize well-cooked meats served with vegetables allowed to express their own distinctiveness rather than wallowing in heavy sauces. Look elsewhere if you're craving wildly creative flavor combinations, but if you like simple, well-prepared food, Rancho Pinot may be the place. You might start with grilled squid salad with preserved lemon and then move on to a house specialty, Nonni's chicken, braised with white wine, mushrooms, and herbs, or a handmade pasta. There's a short but well-chosen list of beers and wines by the glass, and for dessert, delectably rich homemade ice cream. The staff is friendly and tends to treat you as though you were a regular even if it's your first visit.

Razz's Restaurant and Bar. 10321 N. Scottsdale Rd. (in the Windmill Plaza). ☎ **480/905-1308.** Reservations recommended. Main courses $17–$24. AE, DC, MC, V. Tues–Sat 5–10pm. INTERNATIONAL.

Razz Kamnitzer, a native Venezuelan, is one in a line of seven chefs in his family. No wonder his restaurant is such a hit. Located in a nondescript shopping mall on the southeast corner of Shea Boulevard and Scottsdale Road, the restaurant is chic, but not stuffy, crowded, and lively. Razz has been on the Phoenix restaurant scene for some years and is known for his cuisine, which includes edible flowers, herbs, and exotic vegetable and fruits. On a recent night, the menu included such wide-ranging dishes as twice-roasted duck breast with berry-orange sauce; an Indonesian-style noodle dish with chicken, shrimp, pork, and vegetables; and grilled rack of lamb with tamarind and garlic marinade.

✪ **Restaurant Hapa.** 6204 N. Scottsdale Rd. (behind Trader Joes). ☎ **480/998-8220.** Reservations recommended. Main courses $16–$29; small plates $6–$16. AE, MC, V. Mon–Sat 5:30–10pm. PAN ASIAN.

This small and somewhat intimate space is popular with all ages and features a Zen decor, with huge mirrors covering one wall. They have a way with a grill here that really brings out the flavor of shrimp and fish and also turns out some excellent grilled vegetables. From the depths of the wood-burning oven come such dishes as game hen and deftly prepared fish with roasted vegetables. We like the strong flavor combinations on the small plates a lot: spicy squid salad in a chili-lemongrass sauce; shrimp, quail, and chicken satay with three sauces; and pork and ginger potstickers with curried mustard sauce. To round out this Asian-American eating experience, try a delicious dessert such as warm chocolate mango cake with lemongrass ice cream and mango fruit sauce, a melting mélange of contrasting flavors. An adjoining sushi lounge is open during the same hours as the restaurant.

✪ **Roaring Fork.** 7243 E. Camelback Rd. ☎ **480/947-0795.** Reservations highly recommended. Main courses $14–$25. AE, MC, V. Mon–Sat 5:30–10pm. SOUTHWESTERN.

This trendy and very Southwestern restaurant, near the intersection of Camelback and Scottsdale roads, is the creation of chef Robert McGrath, formerly of The Phoenician's Windows on the Green. With its stone walls, mélange of Mexican hacienda and Italian villa architectural styles, and impeccably upscale Southwestern interior, Roaring Fork is a much more casual space than Windows on the Green, yet the cuisine is just as creative. Just be sure you try the sugar-chile glazed duck breast with green chile macaroni (a house specialty). Filled with herb-infused rolls and corn muffins accompanied by honey-chile butter, the bread basket alone is enough to make you weep with joy. There may not be any chilies in the desserts, but they're still worth saving room for. If you can't get a table, it's no disappointment to dine at the bar, since the rebar lariats there hold bowls of bar munchies, including pieces of spicy jerky. And don't miss the huckleberry margaritas. Robert McGrath takes a very hands-on approach with his restaurant—you might see him waiting tables and checking with diners to be sure that they're enjoying their meals.

✪ **Roy's of Scottsdale.** 7001 N. Scottsdale Rd, at the Scottsdale Seville. ☎ **480/905-1155.** Reservations recommended. Main courses $16.50–$27; smaller plates $7–$11. AE, MC, V. Sun–Thurs 5–10pm; Fri–Sat 5–11pm. EURO-ASIAN.

So you decided to go to Arizona instead of Hawaii this year, but you really prefer pan-Asian flavors to those of the Southwest.

Don't worry—even in Scottsdale you can now get Hawaiian chef Roy Yamaguchi's patented pan-Asian cuisine. Brilliant combinations and flamboyant presentations are the hallmark here, and despite lively atmosphere, service usually runs like clockwork. The menu includes nightly specials such as an unusual fried spicy tuna roll or wood-fired tiger shrimp and bacon pizza. Signature entrees include blackened ahi tuna with a hot soy-mustard sauce and meatloaf with wild-mushroom gravy. If you can't get a reservation, you can usually get seats at the counter, which provides a great floor show of cooks preparing food at lightning speed. From the counter, you can also see what's being made and order dishes that look tempting. Desserts are both delicious and beautifully sculpted.

There's another Roy's at 24th Street and Camelback Road in the Camelback Esplanade (☎ **602/381-1155**).

6th Avenue Bistrot. 7150 E. 6th Ave. ☎ **480/947-6022.** Reservations recommended. Main courses $7.25–$12.50 at lunch, $15–$22 at dinner. AE, MC, V. Sun–Mon 5–9pm; Tues–Thurs 11am–2pm and 5–9pm; Fri–Sat 11am–2pm and 5–10pm. CLASSIC FRENCH.

Who says French has to be fussy? This little bistro less than a block off Scottsdale Road is as casual as a French restaurant gets (although it's a bit more formal in the evening). The draw here is a simple menu of reliable dishes at fairly reasonable prices: a bit of country pâté, tenderloin of pork with port-wine sauce, a hearty Beaujolais, all topped off with *mousse au chocolat,* and you have a perfect French dinner. Lunch here is a great deal, and wines by the glass are reasonably priced.

Sushi Ko. 9301 E. Shea Blvd. #126 (in the Mercado del Rancho shopping plaza). ☎ **480/860-2960.** Reservations recommended for dinner. Main courses $5–$10 at lunch, $7–$19 at dinner. AE, DC, DISC, MC, V. Mon–Fri 11:30am–2pm and 5:30–10pm; Sat–Sun 5:30–10pm. JAPANESE.

Recommended by those who know good sushi and popular with the Japanese community, Sushi Ko is a little restaurant in a shopping plaza not far from both the Fairmont Scottsdale Princess and the Hyatt Regency Scottsdale Resort. What makes this place stand out, in addition to the fresh and well-prepared sushi, are the unusual items that appear on the sushi menu—fresh sardine sushi, monk fish pâté, *Edamame* (steamed and salted soybeans that you pop from the shell and eat), and dynamite green mussels (mussels baked with mushrooms and mayonnaise; sounds strange but tastes great).

Table-side cooking is a specialty here, and you can get *shabu-shabu,* a hotpot dish of thinly sliced beef and vegetables served with ponzu sauce.

Veneto Trattoria Italiana. 6137 N. Scottsdale Rd. (in Hilton Village). ☎ **480/948-9928.** Reservations recommended. Main courses $8–$22. AE, CB, DC, DISC, MC, V. Mon–Sat 11:30am–2:30pm and 5–10pm. VENETIAN ITALIAN.

This casual and pleasantly low-key bistro, specializing in the cuisine of Venice, serves simple and satisfying "peasant food" (surprising, because the owner formerly ran the restaurant at the Giorgio Armani boutique in Beverly Hills). A salad of thinly sliced smoked beef, shaved parmesan, and arugula greens, or tender calamari rings served over spinach and savoy cabbage make great starters, followed by *luganega con verzette e polenta,* a lightly spiced sausage with perfectly prepared polenta. *Baccala mantecato* (creamy fish mousse on grilled polenta, made with dried salt cod soaked in milk overnight) may sound unusual, but it's heavenly—for this alone we would recommend the restaurant. For a finale, the *semifreddo con frutta secca,* a partially frozen meringue with dry fruits in a pool of raspberry sauce, has an intoxicating texture. There's outdoor seating on the patio (you can almost forget you're in a shopping mall) and a welcoming bistro ambience inside.

INEXPENSIVE

✪ **Bandera.** 3821 N. Scottsdale Rd., Scottsdale. ☎ **480/994-3524.** Reservations not accepted. Main courses $10–$23. AE, DISC, MC, V. Sun–Thurs 4:30–10pm; Fri–Sat 4:30–11pm. AMERICAN.

If you spent all day wandering in and out of Scottsdale galleries without buying a single bronze statue, you just might be a frugal traveler. If so, you'll want to know about Bandera. Actually, if you've been craving barbecue or grilled chicken for a few hours, chances are it's because you've been smelling the wood-roasted chickens turning on the rotisseries in Bandera's back-of-the-building, open-air stone oven. What an aroma! The succulent spit-roasted chicken is served with the ultimate comfort food, a mountain of creamy mashed potatoes flecked with green onion and black pepper. Sure, you could order prime rib, clams, or leg of lamb, but you'd be a fool if you did. Stick with the chicken or maybe the honey-barbecued ribs, and you won't go wrong. The succulent smoked salmon appetizer is also a hit. This place may be a California chain, but, hey, Californians know good food.

Carlsbad Tavern. 3313 N. Hayden Rd., Scottsdale (south of Osborn). ☎ **480/970-8164.** Reservations recommended at dinner. Main courses $7–$19. AE, DC, DISC, MC, V. Mon–Sat 11am–1am; Sun 1pm–1am; limited menu available from 10 or 11pm until 1am. NEW MEXICAN.

Carlsbad Tavern blends the fiery tastes of New Mexican cuisine with a hip and humorous atmosphere featuring bats (a reference to Carlsbad Caverns). On the menu you'll find traditional New Mexican dishes, such as lamb *pierna* and *carne adovada,* simmered in a fiery red chili sauce. Nouvelle Southwestern specialties include a spicy peppercorn cream–sauced pasta with grilled chicken, andouille sausage, and pine nuts, and a robust chorizo meatloaf sandwich. Cool off your taste buds with a margarita made with fresh-squeezed juice. A lagoon makes this place feel like a beach bar, and a big patio fireplace is really cozy on a cold night.

El Guapo's Taco Shop & Salsa Bar. 3015 N. Scottsdale Rd., Scottsdale (in Plaza 777). ☎ **480/423-8385.** Main dishes $2–$8. No credit cards. Mon–Sat 10:30am–8pm. MEXICAN.

El Guapo means "handsome," which certainly doesn't refer to this little hole-in-the-wall taco shop, but might be referring to Danny, the proprietor. The tacos—among them mahimahi, *carne asada,* or marinated pork—are prepared without the standard lettuce and tomatoes so that you can build your own by liberally dousing your order with salsa and vegetable toppings from the salsa cart. It takes two or three tacos to make a meal, so you can try a few different types. El Guapo has homemade-style cheese crisps, burritos, and nachos, too. Try the armadillo eggs—jalapeño peppers stuffed with cheese and deep-fried. There are only half a dozen tables here, and the salsa bar takes up a good part of the shop.

El Paso Barbeque Company. 8220 N. Hayden Rd. ☎ **480/998-2626.** Main courses $6–$17. AE, DISC, MC, V. Sun–Thurs 11am–10pm; Fri–Sat 11am–11pm. BARBECUE.

This is barbecue Scottsdale style, with an upscale cowboy decor and a bar with two noisy TVs that can make for difficult conversation. But hey, if you're not in a romantic mood, this place is worth the trip for some lip-smacking barbecue, which runs the gamut from ribs to smoked chicken to more uptown barbecued salmon and prime rib. The pulled pork with a smoky sauce and fresh coleslaw is scrumptious. There's also a wide variety of sandwiches, which makes this a good lunch spot or place to get carryout. Want to dine on the lighter side? Order the smoked salmon salad.

Oregano's Pizza Bistro. 3622 N. Scottsdale Rd. (south of Indian School Rd.). ☎ **480/970-1860.** Reservations not accepted. Main courses $5–$17. AE, DC, DISC, MC, V. Mon–Thurs 11am–10pm; Fri–Sat 11am–11pm; Sun noon–10pm. PIZZA/PASTA.

With very reasonable prices and a location convenient to the many shops and galleries of Old Scottsdale, this sprawling pizza joint (two buildings and the courtyard/parking lot between) is a big hit with the area's young crowd. Both the thin-crust pizzas—topped with barbecue chicken and feta cheese (too much for one person, by the way)—and the Chicago stuffed pizza are all the good things pizza should be. In addition to pizza, the menu includes artichoke lasagna, barbecued wings, a variety of salads, and even a pizza cookie for dessert. Because this is such a popular spot, expect a wait at dinner.

Other locations: in Phoenix, 130 E. Washington St. (☎ **602/ 253-9577**), and in Tempe, 523 W. University Dr. (☎ **480/858-0501**).

2 North Scottsdale, Carefree & Cave Creek

EXPENSIVE

La Hacienda. At the Fairmont Scottsdale Princess Resort, 7575 E. Princess Dr. (about 12 miles north of downtown Scottsdale). ☎ **480/585-4848.** Reservations recommended. Main courses $22–$30. AE, CB, DC, DISC, MC, V. Daily 6–10pm. GOURMET MEXICAN.

As you might have guessed by the price range above, this is not your average taco stand. La Hacienda serves gourmet Mexican cuisine in an upscale, glamorous-but-rustic setting reminiscent of an early 1900s Mexican ranch house (stone-tiled floor, Mexican glassware and crockery, a beehive fireplace). Gourmet Mexican means such dishes as the signature suckling pig stuffed with chorizo sausage, or rack of lamb unlike any you may have had before—with a pumpkin-seed crust and chili-plum sauce. Live music nightly adds to the lively atmosphere at this place.

✪ **Marquesa.** At the Fairmont Scottsdale Princess Resort, 7575 E. Princess Dr. (about 12 miles north of downtown Scottsdale). ☎ **480/585-4848.** Reservations recommended. Main courses $29–$41; champagne brunch $47. AE, CB, DC, DISC, MC, V. Tues–Thurs 6–10pm; Fri–Sat 6–11pm; Sun brunch 10:30am–2:30pm. MEDITERRANEAN/CATALAN.

The Marquesa is as romantic a restaurant as you're likely to find in the valley: High-backed chairs, chandeliers, muted lighting, and large classical Spanish paintings create an ambience reminiscent of an 18th-century Spanish villa. The menu is a contemporary interpretation of Catalonian (regional Spanish) with Italian, French, Greek, and Moroccan influences. Lobster cakes with a morel mushroom fondue make for a robustly flavored starter. *Paella Valenciana,* which is the restaurant's signature dish and includes such ingredients as lobster, frog legs, mussels, shrimp, cockles, and fragrant saffron rice, should not be missed. Among the caloric works of art called dessert you might find a crème fraîche flan with roasted pears. The Sunday "market-style" brunch here is one of the best in the valley.

Michael's. 8700 E. Pinnacle Peak Rd. (at the Citadel). ☎ **480/515-2575.** Reservations recommended. Main courses $18–$26. AE, DC, MC, V. Mon–Sat 11am–2:30pm and 6–10pm; Sun 10am–2:30pm (brunch) and 6–10pm. CONTEMPORARY AMERICAN/INTERNATIONAL.

Located in the Citadel shopping/business plaza in north Scottsdale, Michael's was once a remote culinary outpost. However, as Scottsdale's upscale suburbs have marched ever northward, the city has bulldozed its way to Michael's doorstep. Push through the restaurant's front door, and you'll find out exactly why foodies are willing to make the drive out here. The setting is simple yet elegant, which allows the drama of food presentation to take the fore. Picture dishes such as mushroom strudel with poached prawns in a red pepper sauce; bacon-wrapped pork médaillons on baked Asian pears with lemongrass demi-glace; or grilled loin of lamb on a goat cheese and potato tart. Don't miss the "silver spoons" hors d'oeuvres—tablespoons each containing three or four ingredients that burst with flavors. Throughout the year, Chef Michael partners with other local chefs to present special themed lunches and dinners. Call ☎ **480/515-3550** for information.

Restaurant Oceana. 8900 E. Pinnacle Peak Rd. (at Pima Rd.), La Mirada shopping center. ☎ **480/515-2277.** Reservations recommended. Main courses $19–$36. AE, DC, DISC, MC, V. Mon–Thurs 5:30–9pm; Fri–Sat 5:30–10pm. Also open for dinner Sun during winter. SEAFOOD.

North Scottsdale seems to be where the action is these days when it comes to new resorts, golf courses, posh suburbs, and restaurants. Among the best of the latter is a rather small seafood restaurant in an attractive shopping center that has no less than four upscale restaurants. As the name implies, Oceana specializes in all things finny, plus plenty of crustaceans; everything is as fresh as it can be here in the middle of the desert. A wood oven and a sushi bar guarantee that the restaurant will appeal to a wide variety of palates. However, standouts well worth trying include the wood-oven baked mussels, the house-smoked salmon, the grilled-rare ahi tuna, and the Dungeness crab cakes. When it comes time for dessert, be sure to order a sampler plate.

3 Central Phoenix & the Camelback Corridor

EXPENSIVE

Christopher's Fermier Brasserie and Paola's Wine Bar. 2584 E. Camelback Rd. (in Biltmore Fashion Park). ☎ **602/522-2344.** Reservations recommended. Main courses $9–$11 at lunch, $17–$30 at dinner. AE, DISC, MC, V. Mon–Thurs 11am–3pm and 5–10pm; Fri 11am–3pm and 5–11pm; Sat noon–3pm and 5–11pm; Sun noon–3pm and 5–10pm. RUSTIC FRENCH.

Christopher Gross's venue in Biltmore Fashion Park covers many bases. There's a wine bar, a brewery, a cigar room, and a restaurant. Tasty standouts in the restaurant include a velvety roasted–red bell pepper soup with truffle essence and the house-smoked salmon, both holdovers from Gross's previous restaurant. Duck cassoulet with Merguez sausage was remarkably uninteresting. The brewery produces a wide range of beer styles; to give them all a try, order a flight. We prefer the darker ones. A wine bar menu is served from 3 to 5pm, when you can nibble on such things as smoked chicken pizza, French and California cheeses with wine, or Gross's signature dessert, a chocolate mousse tower.

Coup des Tartes. 4626 N. 16th St. ☎ **602/212-1082.** Reservations recommended. Main courses $14–$19. AE, DISC, MC, V. Tues–Sat 5:30–9:30pm. FRENCH.

Chain restaurants, theme restaurants, restaurants that are all style and little substance. Sometimes in Phoenix, it seems impossible to find a genuinely homey little hole-in-the-wall restaurant that serves good food. Coupe des Tartes, only 2 blocks off Camelback Road yet easy to miss, is just such a hole in the wall. With barely a dozen tables and no liquor license (bring your own wine), Coupe des Tartes is about as removed from the standard Phoenix glitz as you can get without getting on a plane and leaving town. The food is primarily rustic French to go with the casual atmosphere. Start your meal with pate de campagne or brie brûlée, which is covered with caramelized apples. The entree menu is always quite short, but you might opt for a lemon-herb encrusted pork tenderloin with chèvre mashed potatoes or filet mignon with a prosciutto-mushroom sauce. For dessert, don't miss the banana brûlée tart.

Eddie Matney's. 2398 E. Camelback Rd. ☎ **602/957-3214.** Reservations recommended. Main courses $9–$14 at lunch, $15–$25 at dinner. AE, DISC, MC, V. Mon–Thurs 11:30am–2:30pm and 5–10:30pm; Fri 11:30am–2:30pm and 5–11:30pm; Sat 5–11:30pm; Sun 5–10:30pm. CONTEMPORARY AMERICAN.

Eddie Matney has been on the Phoenix restaurant scene for quite a few years now and continues to keep local foodies happy with his mix of creativity and comfort. This current restaurant is an upscale bistro in a glass office tower at Camelback Road's most upscale corner, which means it is a popular power lunch and business dinner spot but also works well for a romantic evening out. The menu ranges far and wide for inspiration and features everything from Eddie's famous meatloaf to trout wrapped in grape leaves and topped with four-onion marmalade. There are plenty of Southwestern and Mediterranean influences on the menu here, and the lunch menu is almost as creative as the dinner menu (but at lower prices).

Harris'. 3101 E. Camelback Rd. ☎ **602/508-8888.** Reservations highly recommended. Main courses $8–$19 at lunch, $17–$32 at dinner. AE, DC, DISC, MC, V. Mon–Fri 11:30am–2pm and 5:30–10pm; Sat 5:30–10pm. STEAKS.

If you haven't noticed yet, beef is back in a big way. Enormous slabs of steak, perfectly cooked and allowed to express their inner beefiness unsullied by silly sauces are de rigueur from Manhattan to Marin County these days, and no longer is it necessary to visit some steakhouse that has aged longer than the meat it serves. Today steaks are being served in settings once reserved for various incarnations of nouvelle cuisine.

Harris', smack in the middle of the bustling big-money Camelback Corridor, is one of Phoenix's biggest contemporary steakhouses and popular with wealthy retirees. With a Southwestern pueblo-modern styling, valet parking attendants, and prime rib a specialty of the house, this impressive restaurant leaves no doubt that this is where you'll find your beef. Make sure you've got plenty of space left on your credit card—a meal here will definitely set you back some bucks. At lunch (when prices are lower), the New York steak salad with bleu cheese and candied pecans fairly snaps with flavor—ask for it if you don't see it on the menu.

✪ **Lon's.** At the Hermosa Inn, 5532 N. Palo Cristi Rd. ☎ **602/955-7878.** Reservations recommended late in the week. Main courses $8–$13 at lunch, $18–$27 at dinner. AE, CB, DISC, MC, V. Mon–Fri 11:30am–2pm and 6–10pm; Sat 6–10pm; Sun 10am–2pm (brunch) and 6–10pm. AMERICAN REGIONAL.

What we like most about this place is the setting. It's one of the most "Arizonan" places in the Phoenix area—a Mexican-style hacienda with tile roof and gardens all around. The hacienda once belonged to Lon Megargee, a cowboy artist whose paintings decorate the interior of the restaurant. At midday this place is popular with both retirees and the power-lunching set, and at dinner the place really bustles with a wide mix of people, including smart young things. Begin with rosemary-infused sourdough rolls and a large platter of fried sweet potatoes and red onion rings, which are delicious—salty-sweet and crispy. Dinner entrees are beautifully presented works of art, blending subtle flavors such as grilled salmon with fennel and leeks or pan-seared tiger prawns with watercress sauce. There's a great selection of wines by the glass, a little on the pricey side, and an emphasis on after-dinner drinks. The little bar is cozy and romantic, and the patio offers beautiful views of Camelback Mountain.

Roxsand. 2594 E. Camelback Rd. ☎ **602/381-0444.** Reservations recommended. Main courses $9–$13 at lunch, $19–$26 at dinner. AE, DC, DISC, MC, V. Mon–Thurs 11am–3pm and 5–10pm; Fri–Sat 11am–3pm and 5–11pm; Sun noon–3pm and 5–9:30pm. NEW AMERICAN/FUSION.

Located on the second floor of the exclusive Biltmore Fashion Park shopping mall, Roxsand is a place of urban sophistication, a restaurant at which to see and be seen. Here you'll find fusion cuisine, a creative combination of international influences. We attempted to choose among Moroccan *b'stilla* (braised chicken in phyllo with roasted-eggplant puree), African spicy shrimp salad, and curried lamb tamale. And those were just the appetizers. Sauces sometimes lack complexity, but we can recommend the air-dried duck with pistachio onion marmalade, buckwheat crêpes, and three sauces: Szechuan black-bean sauce, evil jungle prince sauce, and plum sauce. After dinner, get some exercise and amble over to the awesome dessert case; your choice will be served to you on a dinner plate adorned with additional cookies and perhaps a dollop of sorbet.

✪ **T. Cook's.** In the Royal Palms Resort, 5200 E. Camelback Rd. ☎ **602/808-0766.** Reservations highly recommended. Main courses $12–$16 at lunch, $19–$29 at dinner. AE, DC, DISC, MC, V. Mon–Sat 6am–2pm and 5:30–10pm; Sun 10am–2pm (brunch) and 5:30–10pm. MEDITERRANEAN.

Simply put, there is no restaurant in the Valley of the Sun more romantic than T. Cook's. Located within the walls of the Mediterranean-inspired Royal Palms resort, this restaurant is surrounded by decades-old gardens and even has palm trees growing right through the roof of the dining room. The focal point of T. Cook's open kitchen is a wood-fired oven that produces dishes such as spit-roasted chicken and rosemary pork loin with fig-apple chutney and garlic mashed potatoes. However, dishes that don't originate in the wood oven, such as the sautéed lobster with fresh tortellini and asparagus are also worth considering. T. Cook's continues to make big impressions right through to the dessert course. If you happen to be a chocoholic, you'll find nirvana in the chocolate sampler, a collection of confectionery sculptures guaranteed to dazzle the eye as well as satisfy the primordial need for chocolate. Although this is one of the most popular upper-end restaurants in Phoenix these days, it luckily manages to avoid pretentiousness.

✪ **Vincent Guerithault on Camelback.** 3930 E. Camelback Rd. ☎ **602/224-0225.** Reservations highly recommended. Main courses $8.75–$12.50 at lunch, $16–$29 at dinner. AE, DC, MC, V. Mon–Fri 11:30am–2:30pm and 6–10pm; Sat 5:30–10pm. SOUTHWESTERN.

Vincent Guerithault has long been a local restaurant celebrity, and his restaurant has an intimate, unpretentious French country atmosphere. Despite the continental decor, the cuisine is solidly Southwestern, with chilies appearing in numerous guises. For a starter, it's hard to beat the aggressive flavors of a smoked-salmon quesadilla with dill and horseradish cream. Moving on to the main course, grilled meats and seafood are the specialty here and might come accompanied by a cilantro salsa or by habañero pasta. The extensive wine list has both Californian and French wines. There's a parking attendant at the door, and the number of luxury cars here should tip you off that this is one of Phoenix's top restaurants. At lunch, the menu is basically the same as at dinner (only with smaller portions). With nearly all items at about $10, lunchtime is a great opportunity to taste the food if you're on a budget.

MODERATE

Altos. 5029 N. 44th St. (at the NE corner of 44th St. and Camelback). ☎ **602/808-0890.** Reservations recommended. Main courses $19–$23; tapas $8–$12. AE, MC, V. Sun–Thurs 5:30–10pm; Fri–Sat 5:30–11pm. CONTEMPORARY SPANISH.

Well hidden in the back of a Camelback Road shopping plaza, Altos is a little difficult to find, but it's definitely worth searching out. It's a casually chic place to enjoy a light meal of *tapas* (small dishes) and sangria, although more substantial dishes are also quite good. Contemporary and classic treatments of Spanish food are the specialty here, including tapas such as mussels in sherry sauce or sautéed shrimp with almonds. Paella with seafood, chicken, Basque sausage, and saffron rice is a complex melding of flavors, while some dishes are more straightforward, such as the *pinchitos* (kebabs). Brandy bread pudding or espresso crème brûlée rounds out the experience, along with live flamenco guitar on weekends. There's also salsa dancing now on Wednesday nights in the restaurant's little loft bar.

C-Fu Fine Asian Dining. 3113 E. Lincoln Dr. (in the Biltmore area) ☎ **602/808-9899.** Reservations recommended on weekends. Dishes $9–$20. AE, DC, DISC, MC, V. Mon–Thurs 11am–3pm and 5–10pm; Fri 11am–3pm and 5–11pm; Sat noon–3pm and 5–11pm; Sun 5–10pm. CHINESE/JAPANESE.

For years the valley has loved C-Fu; the only problem was that the restaurant was way out in Chandler. Now C-Fu is also in Phoenix, less than a mile from the Arizona Biltmore, and with the new location has come a more up-to-date spin on Chinese food. Dishes here are creative and interesting, blending Chinese cuisine with a bit of contemporary American.

There's also a sushi bar thrown in for good measure. Considerable *feng shui* went into the designing of the stylishly contemporary interior, which is quite serene. There are also huge fish tanks showcasing both decorative and edible fish. Tasty standouts on the Chinese menu include a sublime shrimp and mango platter, crab meat in cream sauce over snow pea leaves, and grilled pork tenderloin Beijing style. For dessert, we like the banana *lumpia,* a banana wrapped up like an egg roll and fried.

Richardson's. 1582 E. Bethany Home Rd. ☎ **602/265-5886** or 602/230-8718. Reservations accepted only for parties of 4 or more. Main courses $9–$22. AE, CB, DC, MC, V. Mon–Fri 11am–midnight; Sat–Sun 10am–midnight. NEW MEXICAN.

Tucked into an older corner shopping center with far too few parking spaces, Richardson's is almost invisible amid the glaring lights and flashing neon of this otherwise unmemorable neighborhood. This place isn't touristy or trendy, although it's generally a mob scene at dinner; however, if you enjoy creative, spicy cooking at good prices, it's worth the wait. Have a margarita while you're at it. If you're in the mood for a light meal, try one of the skewers—chicken, beef, shrimp, and sausage grilled over pecan wood. A more substantial appetite may be assuaged by a New Mexican platter containing a tamale, a chile relleno, a burrito, rice and beans, and green chile. The pecan-wood pizza oven is always fired up to cook delicious pizzas, and for dessert, prickly pear–syrup flan is as creamy as a good crème brûlée. Richardson's also serves Southwestern-style breakfasts daily from 10 or 11am until 4pm.

INEXPENSIVE

Blue Burrito Grille. In the Biltmore Plaza, 3118 E. Camelback Rd. ☎ **602/955-9596.** Reservations not accepted. Main courses $4.50–$7. AE, MC, V. Daily 11am–11pm. MEXICAN.

Located in a shopping plaza that also houses the most exclusive and expensive jewelry store in the valley, this is obviously not your usual greasy-tortilla Mexican joint. Catering to a health-conscious affluent community, the Blue Burrito specializes in healthful Mexican food (with no lard and plenty of vegetarian offerings). Okay, so the deep-fried chimichanga isn't good for you, but the chicken fajita burritos, fish tacos, enchiladas rancheras, and tamales Mexicanos certainly are. If you want to blow the healthfulness of your meal, have it with a mango margarita. This is a great place for fast, cheap, healthy food smack in the middle of the Camelback Corridor shopping district. Also in Phoenix at 3815 N. Central Ave. (☎ **602/234-3293**), 7318 E. Shea Blvd. in Scottsdale (☎ **480/951-3151**), and 420 S. Mill St., Tempe (☎ **480/921-1332**).

Ed Debevic's Short Orders Deluxe. 2102 E. Highland Ave. ☎ **602/956-2760.** Reservations not accepted. Sandwiches and blue-plate specials $4.25–$9. AE, DC, DISC, MC, V. Sun–Thurs 11am–9pm; Fri–Sat 11am–10pm. AMERICAN.

Hidden away behind the Smitty's supermarket in the Town and Country Shopping Center, Ed's is a classic 1950s diner right down to the little jukeboxes in the booths. Not only does it make its own burgers, chili, and bread, but Ed Debevic's serves the best malteds in Phoenix. The sign in the front window that reads WAITRESSES WANTED, PEOPLE SKILLS NOT NECESSARY should give you a clue that service here is unique. This place stays busy, and the waitresses are overworked (although they do break into song now and again), so don't be surprised if your waitress sits down in the booth with you to wait for your order. That's just the kind of place Ed runs, and as Ed says, "If you don't like the way I do things—buy me out."

5 & Diner. 5220 N. 16th St. ☎ **602/264-5220.** Sandwiches/plates $5–8. AE, MC, V. Daily 24 hours. AMERICAN.

If it's 2am and you just have to have a big burger and a side of fries after a night of dancing, head for the 24-hour 5 & Diner. You can't miss it; it's the classic streamlined diner that looks as though it just materialized from New Jersey.

There's another location in Paradise Valley at 12802 N. Tatum Blvd. (☎ **602/996-0033**) and one in Scottsdale at Scottsdale Pavilions, 9069 E. Indian Bend Rd. (☎ **480/949-1957**).

Vintage Market. 24th St. and Camelback Rd. (Biltmore Fashion Park). ☎ **602/955-4444.** Reservations not necessary. Salads/sandwiches $7. AE, DC, MC, V. Mon–Wed 10am–7pm; Thurs–Sat 10am–9pm; Sun 11am–6pm. UPSCALE DELI.

This is a prime people-watching spot and a great place for European-style sandwiches, accompanied by strong coffee in demitasse cups or a glass of wine chosen from a long list. There's also a wine bar. Prices here are lower than at practically

Family-Friendly Restaurants

Ed Debevic's Short Orders Deluxe *(see p. 90)* This classic 1950s diner is full of cool stuff, including little jukeboxes in the booths. You can tell your kids about hanging out in places like this when you were a teenager.

Pinnacle Peak Patio *(see p. 96)* Way out in north Scottsdale, this restaurant is a Wild West steakhouse complete with cowboys, shoot-outs, hayrides, and live Western music nightly.

Rawhide Western Town & Steakhouse *(see p. 96)* Kids love dancing to the country music and pretending they're in a real Old West town, which isn't difficult, since Rawhide, with its big wide street, looks pretty authentic. Did you know they cook up 50 *tons* of beans here annually?

Rustler's Rooste *(see p. 97)* Similar to Pinnacle Peak, but closer to the city center, Rustler's Rooste has a slide from the lounge to the main dining room, a big patio, and live cowboy bands nightly. See if you can get your kids to try the rattlesnake appetizer—it tastes like chicken.

any other place in Biltmore Fashion Park, and you can get the likes of a Mediterranean focaccia or Asian vegetable and shrimp salad. Also in Scottsdale at The Borgata, 6166 N. Scottsdale Rd. (☎ **480/315-8199**).

4 Downtown Phoenix

MODERATE

✪ **Sam's Cafe.** In the Arizona Center, 455 N. 3rd St. ☎ **602/252-3545.** Reservations recommended. Main courses $8–$19. AE, CB, DISC, MC, V. Mon–Thurs 11am–10pm; Fri–Sat 11am–11pm; Sun 11am–9pm. SOUTHWESTERN.

Sam's Cafe, one of only a handful of decent downtown restaurants, serves food that's every bit as imaginative, but not nearly as expensive, as that served at other (often overrated) Southwestern restaurants in Phoenix. Breadsticks served with picante-flavored cream cheese, grilled vegetable tacos, and angel-hair pasta in a spicy jalapeño sauce with shrimp and mushrooms all have a nice balance of flavors and are just spicy enough. Salads and dipping sauces are complex and interesting. The downtown Sam's has a large patio that stays packed with the lunchtime, after-work, and convention crowds and overlooks a fountain and palm garden.

Other Sam's restaurants are located in the Biltmore Fashion Park at 2566 E. Camelback Rd. (☎ **602/954-7100**) and in Scottsdale at North Scottsdale Road and Shea Boulevard (☎ **480/368-2800**).

INEXPENSIVE

Alice Cooper'stown. 101 E. Jackson St. ☎ **602/253-7337.** Reservations not accepted. Sandwiches/barbecue $6–$19. AE, MC, V. Daily 11am–11pm. BARBECUE.

Another venue comes to the realm of eat-o-tainment with the opening of Alice Cooper's sports-and-rock theme restaurant located between the Bank One Ballpark and America West Arena. Sixteen video screens are the centerpiece of the restaurant (and most likely they'll be showing sports), but there is also an abundance of memorabilia on the walls, from Alice Cooper's platinum records to guitars from Fleetwood Mac and Eric Clapton to plenty of celebrity photographs. Barbecue occurs in various permutations, from a huge and pretty tasty sandwich to a BBQ Feast platter. There are plenty of other choices too, such as a 2-foot-long hot dog, ribs, and "Megadeth" meatloaf. The waitstaff even wears Alice Cooper makeup.

Honey Bear's BBQ. 2824 N. Central Ave. ☎ **602/279-7911.** Sandwiches and dinners $3.70–$12.50. AE, CB, DC, MC, V. Mon–Sat 10am–10pm; Sun 10am–9:30pm. BARBECUE.

We can definitely say that Honey Bear's has a dud-free menu, and it couldn't be simpler—pork barbecue, beef barbecue, or chicken barbecue. Accompanied maybe by some coleslaw to stick on top of a sandwich or sweet potato pie for dessert. This fast food joint has another location at 5012 E. Van Buren St. (☎ **602/273-9148**).

✪ **MacAlpine's Nostalgic Soda Fountain & Coffee Shoppe.** 2303 N. 7th St. ☎ **602/252-7282.** Sandwiches/specials $3.25–$6. AE, MC, V. Mon–Thurs 7am–3pm; Fri–Sat 7am–11pm; Sun 11am–5pm. AMERICAN.

This very authentic place hasn't changed much since its beginnings in 1928—in fact, it's the oldest operating soda fountain in the Southwest. The atmosphere is laid-back, and wooden booths and worn countertops show the patina of time. They'll be glad to fix you up a breakfast egg on a bagel or a big hamburger or tuna sandwich on good bread. To wash it down, order a chocolate phosphate, raspberry iced tea, or huge iced mocha.

✪ **Pizzeria Bianco.** In Heritage Square, 623 E. Adams St. ☎ **602/258-8300.** Reservations accepted for 6 or more. Pizzas $8–$11. MC, V. Tues–Sat 5–10pm; Sun 5–9pm. ITALIAN.

Even though this historic brick building is located smack dab in the center of downtown Phoenix, the atmosphere is so friendly and cozy it feels like your neighborhood local. The wood-burning oven turns out deliciously rustic, chewy-crusted pizzas, such as one with red onion, Parmesan, rosemary, and crushed pistachio. Pizzeria Bianco makes its own fresh mozzarella cheese, which can be ordered as an appetizer or on a pizza. We also liked the roasted vegetables and the salad with fennel, dandelion greens, and orange, drizzled with olive oil.

5 Tempe, Mesa, South Phoenix & the Airport Area

MODERATE

✪ **House of Tricks.** 114 E. 7th St., Tempe. ☎ **480/968-1114.** Reservations recommended. Main courses $13–$22. AE, CB, DC, DISC, MC, V. Mon–Sat 11am–10pm. Closed first 2 weeks of Aug. NEW AMERICAN.

Because this restaurant is housed in a pair of Craftsman bungalows surrounded by an attractive garden of shady trees, it has a completely different feel from Mill Avenue, Tempe's main drag, which is only 2 blocks away. This is where Arizona State University students take their parents when they come to visit, but it's also a nice spot for a romantic evening and a good place to try innovative cuisine without blowing your vacation budget. The grape arbor–covered patio, where there's also a shady bar, is the preferred seating area. The dinner menu changes regularly and consists of a single page of tempting salads, appetizers, and main dishes. The garlic-inspired Caesar salad and the house-smoked salmon with avocado, capers, and lemon cream are good bets for starters. Among the entrees, look for the pork rack with jalapeño marmalade.

Monti's La Casa Vieja. 1 W. Rio Salado Pkwy. (at the corner of Mill Ave.), Tempe. ☎ **480/967-7594.** Reservations recommended for dinner. Main courses $5–$27. AE, CB, DC, DISC, MC, V. Sun–Thurs 11am–10pm; Fri–Sat 11am–midnight. AMERICAN.

If you're tired of the glitz and glamour of the Valley of the Sun and are looking for Old Arizona, head down to Tempe to Monti's La Casa Vieja. The adobe building was constructed in 1873 (*casa vieja* means "old house" in Spanish) on the site of the Salt River ferry in the days when the Salt River flowed year-round and Tempe was nothing more than a ferry crossing. Today local families who have been in Phoenix for generations know Monti's well and rely on the restaurant for solid meals and low prices—you can get a filet mignon for under $11. The dining rooms are dark and filled with memorabilia of the Old West.

INEXPENSIVE

✪ **The Farm at South Mountain.** 6106 S. 32nd St. Take Exit 151A off I-10 and go south on 32nd St. ☎ **602/276-6360.** Sandwiches and salads $8.50. AE, DC, MC, V. Tues–Sun 8am–3pm (if weather is inclement, call to be sure it's open). SANDWICHES & SALADS.

If being in the desert has you dreaming of shady trees and green grass, you'll enjoy this little oasis reminiscent of a New England orchard or Midwestern farm. A rustic outbuilding surrounded by potted flowers has been converted to a stand-in-line restaurant where you can order a mesquite grilled eggplant sandwich or have a choice of fresh salads such as a pecan turkey Waldorf with sour cream and dried apricot dressing. Breakfast choices are baked goods such as muffins and scones, teas, and juices. The grassy lawn is ideal for a picnic on a blanket under the pecan trees.

Friday and Saturday nights, seven-course gourmet dinners ($55 per person) using garden produce are served at the old farmhouse. Reservations are a necessity; in fact, it's best to call as far ahead as possible. For more information, call **Quiescence** at ☎ **602/305-8192.**

Organ Stop Pizza. 1149 E. Southern Ave., Mesa (southwest corner of Southern Ave. and Stapley Dr.). ☎ **480/813-5700.** Pizza and pastas $4.50–$14. Credit cards not accepted. Sun–Thurs 4–9pm; Fri–Sat 4–10pm. PIZZA.

The pizza here may not be the best in town, but the Mighty Würlitzer theater organ, the largest in the world, sure is memorable. The massive instrument contains over 5,500 pipes, and four turbine blowers provide the wind to create the sound. Forty-foot ceilings make for great acoustics. Performances begin at 4:30pm and continue throughout the evening. As you marvel at skill of the organist, who performs songs ranging from "Livin' la Vida Loca" to "The Phantom of the Opera," you can enjoy simple pizzas, pastas, or snack foods such as nachos or onion rings.

6 Dining with a View

Different Pointe of View. At the Pointe Hilton Tapatio Cliffs Resort, 11111 N. 7th St. ☎ **602/863-0912.** Reservations highly recommended. Main courses $26–$36. AE, CB, DC, DISC, MC, V. Mon–Thurs 5:30–9:30pm; Fri–Sat 5:30–10pm (lounge open later); Sun 5:30–9:30pm. REGIONAL AMERICAN.

Built right into a mountaintop, this restaurant takes in dramatic, sweeping vistas of the city, mountains, and desert through its curving walls of glass. Come early, and you can enjoy views to the north from the lounge before heading into the south-facing dining room. The menu changes regularly but is always dependable (herb-crusted rack of lamb with sweet potato fries; sautéed shrimp and sea scallops with lobster sherry sauce). However, despite the excellent food, award-winning wine list, and live jazz Wednesday through Saturday, the view steals the show.

✪ **Top of the Rock.** At Wyndham Buttes Resort, 2000 Westcourt Way, Tempe. ☎ **602/225-9000.** Reservations recommended. Main courses $21–$30; Sun brunch $35. AE, CB, DC, DISC, MC, V. Sun–Thurs 5–10pm; Fri–Sat 5–11pm; Sun 10am–2pm (brunch) and 5–10pm. CONTEMPORARY AMERICAN/SOUTHWESTERN.

All the best views in Phoenix are from resorts and their restaurants, so if you want to dine with a view of the valley, you're going to have to pay the price. Luckily, quality accompanies the high prices here at the Top of the Rock, which is built into a rocky hillside and has a dramatic desert setting above Tempe. In addition to the stunning, romantic setting, you can enjoy some very creative cuisine. On the appetizer list, the lobster Napoleon (lobster layered with wonton and Boursin cheese in a white-wine-chervil butter sauce) should not be missed. Sauces on the entree menu offer a good range of flavors from mellow to bold. The ambience is a little on the formal side, so dress up for this dining experience. You won't go wrong ordering any dessert made with chocolate.

7 Cowboy Steakhouses

Although Arizona doesn't claim to have invented the steakhouse or cow towns, the state certainly has cornered the market on combining the two. Wild West theme restaurants abound here in the Phoenix area. These family restaurants generally provide big portions of grilled steaks and barbecued ribs, outdoor and "saloon" dining, live country music, and various sorts of entertainment, including stagecoach rides and shootouts in the street.

Pinnacle Peak Patio. 10426 E. Jomax Rd., Scottsdale. Take Scottsdale Rd. north to Pinnacle Peak Rd., turn right and continue to Pima Rd., turn left and follow the signs. ☎ **480/585-1599.** Reservations recommended on weekends. Main courses $12.50–$25 (children's menu $3–$6). DC, DISC, MC, V. Mon–Thurs 4–10pm; Fri–Sat 4–11pm; Sun noon–10pm. STEAK.

Businessmen beware! Wear a tie into this restaurant, and you'll have it cut off and hung from the rafters (there's somewhere around a quarter million ties hangin' up there). Although you can indulge in mesquite-broiled steaks (they even have a 2-lb. porterhouse monster) with all the traditional trimmings, a meal here is more an event than just an opportunity to put on the feedbag. The real draw is all the free Wild West entertainment—gunfights, cowboy bands, two-stepping, and cookouts. Also of interest are the museum-like displays of interesting collections such as can openers, police badges, and license plates. Although Pinnacle Peak Patio is strictly Hollywood Western, it is now surrounded by the valley's poshest suburbs.

✪ **Rawhide Western Town & Steakhouse.** 23023 N. Scottsdale Rd. (4 miles north of Bell Rd.), Scottsdale. ☎ **480/502-5600.** Reservations accepted for parties of 9 or more. Main courses $8–$12 at lunch, $12–$23 at dinner. AE, CB, DC, DISC, MC, V. Oct–May Mon–Thurs 5–10pm, Fri–Sun 11:30am–3pm and 5–10pm; Apr daily 11:30am–3pm and 5–10pm; May–Sept daily 5–10pm. Lunch served Oct–Mar Fri–Sun 11:30am–3pm and Apr daily 11:30am–3pm. STEAKS.

Sure it's a tourist trap, but Rawhide is so much fun and such a quintessentially Phoenician experience that it's one of our favorite valley restaurants. There's plenty of entertainment, including country-music bands, shootouts, stagecoach rides, a petting zoo, and a resident magician. Kids love pretending they're in a real old Western town, which isn't difficult since Rawhide, with its big wide street, looks pretty authentic. Along with mesquite-broiled steaks, including not only beef but buffalo as well, you'll find a few barbecue items and fruit pie à la mode. They get a lot of visitors here, as evidenced by the fact the kitchen cooks up about 200,000 pounds of steak and 50 tons of beans annually.

Rustler's Rooste. At the Pointe Hilton on South Mountain, 7777 S. Pointe Hwy., Phoenix. ☎ **602/431-6474.** Reservations recommended. Main courses $13–$32. AE, CB, DC, DISC, MC, V. Sun–Thurs 5–10pm; Fri–Sat 5–11pm. STEAKS.

This location doesn't exactly seem like cowboy country. However, up at the top of the hill you'll find a fun Western-theme restaurant where you can slide from the bar down to the main dining room. The view north across Phoenix is entertainment enough for most people, but there are also Western bands playing for those who like to kick up their heels. If you've ever been bitten by a snake, you can exact your revenge here by ordering the rattlesnake appetizer. Follow that (if you've got the appetite of a hardworking cowpoke) with the enormous cowboy "stuff" platter consisting of, among other things, broiled sirloin, barbecued ribs, cowboy beans, fried shrimp, barbecued chicken, and swordfish kebabs.

8 Breakfast, Brunch & Quick Bites

Most of Phoenix's best Sunday brunches are to be had at restaurants in major hotels and resorts. Among the finest are those served at ✪ **Marquesa** (in the Scottsdale Princess), at the **Golden Swan** (in the Hyatt Regency Scottsdale Resort), at **Wright's** (in the Arizona Biltmore Resort & Spa), at the **Terrace Dining Room** (in The Phoenician), and at the **Garden Terrace Restaurant** (in the Doubletree La Posada). For information on the two former restaurants, see "Scottsdale" earlier in this chapter. For information on the latter three restaurants, see chapter 4. The **Desert Botanical Garden,** 1201 N. Galvin Pkwy. (☎ **480/941-1225**), in Papago Park, serves brunch with its Music in the Garden concerts held on Sundays between September and March. Tickets are $13.50 and include admission to the gardens. Sunday brunch is served for an additional charge.

If your idea of the perfect breakfast is a French pastry and a good cup of coffee, try **Pierre's Pastry Café,** 7119 E. Shea Blvd., Scottsdale (☎ **480/443-2510**), where the croissants and brioche have a luxurious, buttery texture (desserts here are also irresistible). Along Camelback Road, in the Biltmore Plaza shopping center, try **La Madeleine,** 3102 E. Camelback Rd. (☎ **602/952-0349**), which is *the* place for a luscious and leisurely French breakfast amid antique French farm implements. The bakery here also does great breads, if you happen to be thinking about a picnic. There's another La Madeleine at Fashion Square Mall, 7014 E. Camelback Rd. (☎ **480/945-1663**) in Scottsdale, and one at Tatum and Shea Boulevards in Paradise Valley (☎ **480/483-0730**).

For fruit smoothies and muffins and healthy things, try **Wild Oats Community Market,** which has stores at 3933 E. Camelback Rd. (☎ **602/954-0584**), in North Phoenix at 13823 N. Tatum Blvd. (☎ **602/953-7546**), and in Scottsdale at 7129 E. Shea Blvd. (☎ **480/905-1441**) at the corner of Scottsdale Road. Almost three dozen different kinds of bagels, plus large, inexpensive delicatessen-style breakfasts can be had at **Chompie's,** 3202 E. Greenway Rd. (☎ **602/971-8010**), 9301 E. Shea Blvd. in the Mercado del Rancho Centre, Scottsdale (☎ **480/860-0475**), and at 1160 E. University Dr., Tempe (☎ **480/557-0700**).

For a quick bite when in downtown Phoenix, the **Gardenside Food Court** at the Arizona Center offers several options.

9 Cafes & Coffee

If you've got a serious coffee habit and want some of the best espresso in the valley, then search out **The Village Coffee Roastery,** 8120 N. Hayden Rd., E104 (☎ **480/905-0881**), in Scottsdale near Franco's Trattoria. The coffee's freshly roasted, and there are lots of shade-grown and organic beans. In Old Town Scottsdale, try **The Author's Café,** 4014 N. Goldwater Blvd. (☎ **480/481-3998**), a stylish little cafe next door to The Poisoned Pen, a mystery bookstore.

6

Seeing the Sights

With its wealth of museums, architectural attractions, shopping opportunities, and outdoor activities, the Valley of the Sun offers something for everyone. This chapter will guide you through the highlights, including how to catch a Phoenix Suns game, where to indulge in a massage, and the best ways to blow $100 on an unforgettable experience.

1 Discovering the Desert & Its Native Cultures

Deer Valley Rock Art Center. 3711 W. Deer Valley Rd. ☎ **623/582-8007.** Admission $4 adults, $2 seniors, $1 children 6–12, free for children 5 and under. Oct–Apr Tues–Sat 9am–5pm, Sun noon–5pm; May–Sept Tues–Fri 8am–2pm, Sat 9am–5pm, Sun noon–5pm. Closed major holidays. Take Deer Valley Rd. exit off I-17 on the north side of Phoenix and go west to just past 35th Ave.

Located in the Hedgepeth Hills in the northwest corner of the Valley of the Sun, the Deer Valley Rock Art Center preserves an amazing concentration of Native American petroglyphs, some of which date back 5,000 years. Although these petroglyphs may not at first seem as impressive as more famous images that have been reproduced ad nauseam in recent years, the sheer numbers make this a fascinating spot. The drawings, which range from simple spirals to much more complex renderings of herds of deer, are on volcanic boulders along a ¼-mile trail. An interpretive center provides background information on this site and on rock art in general.

✪ **Desert Botanical Garden.** Papago Park, 1201 N. Galvin Pkwy. ☎ **480/941-1225.** www.dbg.org. Admission $7.50 adults, $6.50 seniors, $4 students 13–18, $1.50 children 5–12, children under 5 free. Oct–Apr daily 8am–8pm; May–Sept daily 7am–8pm. Closed Dec 25. Bus: 3.

Located adjacent to the Phoenix Zoo and devoted exclusively to cacti and other desert plants, this botanic garden displays more than 20,000 plants from all over the world. The Plants and People of the Sonoran Desert trail is the state's best introduction to ethnobotany (human use of plants) in the

Phoenix, Scottsdale & the Valley of the Sun Attractions

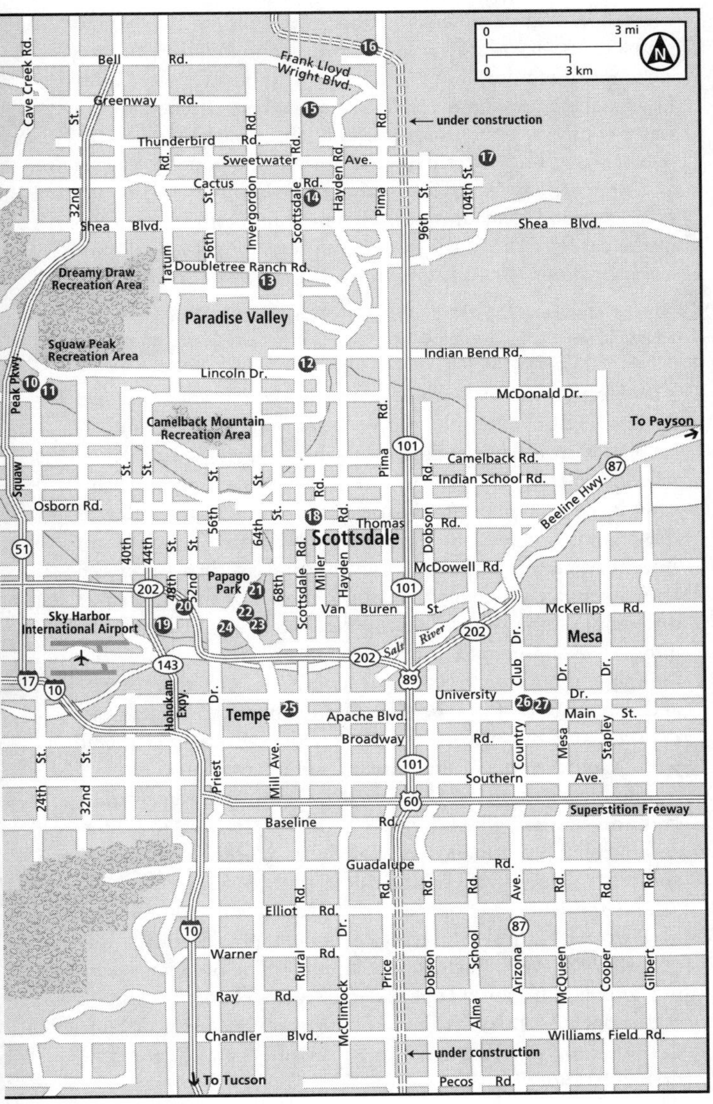

0 3 mi
0 3 km
N
under construction
Frank Lloyd Wright Blvd.
Bell Rd.
Greenway Rd.
Thunderbird Rd.
Sweetwater Ave.
Cactus Rd.
Shea Blvd.
Doubletree Ranch Rd.
Indian Bend Rd.
Lincoln Dr.
McDonald Dr.
Camelback Rd.
Indian School Rd.
Osborn Rd.
Thomas Rd.
McDowell Rd.
Van Buren St.
McKellips Rd.
University Dr.
Main St.
Apache Blvd.
Broadway Rd.
Southern Ave.
Superstition Freeway
Baseline Rd.
Guadalupe Rd.
Elliot Rd.
Warner Rd.
Ray Rd.
Chandler Blvd.
Williams Field Rd.
Pecos Rd.
Cave Creek Rd.
32nd St.
Tatum
56th St.
Invergordon Rd.
Scottsdale Rd.
Hayden Rd.
Pima Rd.
96th St.
104th St.
Squaw Peak Pkwy.
40th St.
44th St.
48th St.
52nd St.
64th St.
68th St.
Miller Rd.
Dobson Rd.
Hohokam Expy.
Priest Dr.
Mill Ave.
Country Club Dr.
Mesa Dr.
Stapley Dr.
24th St.
Rural Rd.
McClintock Dr.
Price Rd.
School Rd.
Alma
Arizona Ave.
McQueen Rd.
Cooper Rd.
Gilbert Rd.
Beeline Hwy.
Salt River
Dreamy Draw Recreation Area
Squaw Peak Recreation Area
Camelback Mountain Recreation Area
Paradise Valley
Scottsdale
Papago Park
Sky Harbor International Airport
Tempe
Mesa
To Payson
To Tucson
10 11 12 13 14 15 16 17 18 19 20 21 22 23 24 25 26 27
17 10 51 202 143 101 89 60 87

Southwest. Along the trail are interactive displays that demonstrate how Native Americans once used wild and cultivated plants. You can make a yucca-fiber brush and practice grinding corn and mesquite beans. At the garden's Center for Desert Living, there are demonstration gardens and an energy- and water-conservation research house. If you come late in the day, you can stay until after dark and see night-blooming flowers and dramatically lit cacti. A cafe on the grounds serves surprisingly good food. In the spring and fall, there are concerts in the garden. The Christmas season sees the gardens illuminated by *luminárias* (candles inside small bags) at night.

✪ **Heard Museum.** 2301 N. Central Ave. ☎ **602/252-8848.** Admission $7 adults, $6 seniors, $3 children 4–12. Daily 9:30am–5pm. Closed major holidays. Bus: Blue (B), Red (R), O.

The Heard Museum is one of the nation's finest museums dealing exclusively with Native American cultures, and as such, it is an ideal introduction to the indigenous cultures of Arizona. **Native Peoples of the Southwest** is an extensive exhibit that examines the culture of each of the major tribes of the region. Included in the exhibit are a Navajo hogan, an Apache wickiup, and a Hopi corn-grinding display. In the large Katsina Doll Gallery you'll get an idea of the number of different kachina spirits that populate the Hopi and Zuni religions. The museum's Crossroads Gallery offers a fascinating look at contemporary Native American art. On many weekends there are performances by Native American singers and dancers, and throughout the week artists demonstrate their work. Guided tours of the museum are offered daily.

The biggest event of the year is the annual spring **Indian Fair and Market,** which is held on the first weekend in March and includes performances of traditional dances as well as arts and crafts demonstrations and sales.

The museum also operates the **Heard Museum North,** El Pedregal Festival Marketplace, 34505 N. Scottsdale Rd. (☎ **480/488-9817**), which is adjacent to The Boulders resort in Carefree. This fairly large gallery features changing exhibits and is open Monday to Saturday 10am to 5:30pm and Sunday noon to 5pm. Admission is $2 for adults and $1 for children ages 4 to 12.

Pueblo Grande Museum & Cultural Park. 4619 E. Washington St. (between 44th St. and 48th St.). ☎ **602/495-0901.** Admission $2 adults,

$1.50 seniors, $1 children 6–17; free on Sun. Mon–Sat 9am–4:45pm; Sun 1–4:45pm. Closed major holidays. Bus: Yellow (Y).

Located near Sky Harbor Airport and downtown Phoenix, the Pueblo Grande Museum and Cultural Park houses the ruins of an ancient Hohokam village. This was one of several villages along the Salt River between A.D. 300 and 1400. Sometime around 1450, this and other villages were mysteriously abandoned. One speculation is that drought and a buildup of salts from irrigation water reduced the fertility of the soil and forced the people to leave their homes and seek more fertile lands. Before touring the grounds to view the partially excavated ruins, you can walk through the small museum, which displays many of the artifacts that have been dug up on the site. The museum sponsors interesting workshops, demonstrations, and tours throughout the year.

2 Museums

ART MUSEUMS

Arizona State University Art Museum. In the Nelson Fine Arts Center, 10th St. and Mill Ave., Tempe. ☎ **480/965-2787.** Free admission. Tues 10am–9pm; Wed–Sat 10am–5pm; Sun 1–5pm. Closed major holidays. Bus: Red (R), Yellow (Y), 66, or 72.

Although it isn't very large, the Arizona State University Art Museum is memorable for its innovative architecture and excellent temporary exhibitions. The building, stark and angular, captures the colors of sunset on desert mountains with its purplish gray stucco facade and pyramidal shape. The museum entrance is down a flight of stairs that leads to a cool underground garden area. Inside are galleries for crafts, prints, contemporary art, Latin American art, a temporary exhibition gallery, two outdoor sculpture courts, and a gift shop. The museum's collection of American art includes works by Georgia O'Keeffe, Edward Hopper, and Frederic Remington.

Fleischer Museum. Perimeter Center, 17207 N. Perimeter Dr. (just north of Frank Lloyd Wright Blvd and east of Hayden Rd.), Scottsdale. ☎ **480/585-3108.** Free admission. Daily 10am–4pm. Closed major holidays.

Located in a modern office park in north Scottsdale, this museum was the country's first gallery dedicated to the California School of American Impressionism, which drew extensively on French Impressionist styles and holds a quiet place in American art history.

✪ **Phoenix Art Museum.** 1625 N. Central Ave. (at the northeast corner of McDowell Rd.). ☎ **602/257-1222.** www.phxart.org. Admission $7 adults, $5 seniors and students, $2 children 6–18, free for children under 6; no admission charge on Thurs. Tues–Wed and Sat–Sun 10am–5pm; Thurs–Fri 10am–9pm. Closed major holidays. Bus: Blue (B), Red (R), O.

This is the largest art museum in the Southwest, and acres of wall space enable it to display canvases of a size rarely seen in museums. Little exhibit halls tucked into out-of-the-way corners, dead-end hallways hung with art, and the museum's two buildings (connected by an enclosed stainless-steel pedestrian bridge) make this a place to spend plenty of time exploring. If you're the linear type, it's easy to completely miss entire exhibit areas here.

Housed within this labyrinth, you'll find a very respectable collection that spans the major artistic movements from the Renaissance to the present. The collection of modern and contemporary art is particularly good, with works by Diego Rivera, Frida Kahlo, Pablo Picasso, Karel Appel, Mark Rothko, Alexander Calder, Henry Moore, Georgia O'Keeffe, Henri Rousseau, and Auguste Rodin.

The large first-floor gallery is used for special exhibits including major touring retrospectives. The Thorne Miniature Collection is one of the museum's most popular exhibits and consists of tiny rooms on a scale of 1 inch to 1 foot. The rooms are exquisitely detailed, right down to the leaded-glass windows of an English lodge kitchen. Other exhibits include decorative arts, historic fashions, Asian art, Spanish colonial furnishings and religious art, and, of course, a Western American exhibit featuring works by members of the Cowboy Artists of America

✪ **Scottsdale Museum of Contemporary Art.** 7380 E. Second St., Scottsdale. ☎ **480/994-ARTS.** Admission $5 adults, $3 students, free for children under 15; no admission charge on Thurs. Tues–Wed and Fri–Sat 10am–5pm; Thurs 10am–9pm; Sun noon–5pm. Bus: 41, 50, 72. Also accessible on Scottsdale Round Up shuttle bus.

Scottsdale may be obsessed with art featuring lonesome cowboys and solemn Indians, but this boldly designed museum makes it clear that patrons of contemporary art are also welcome here. Cutting-edge art, from the abstract to the absurd, fills the galleries here, with exhibits rotating every few months. Shows scheduled in 2001 will feature the work of James Turrell, Donald Sultan, Mary Bates, and Wolfgang Laib. In addition to the galleries in the main museum building, there are several more galleries in the adjacent Scottsdale Center for the Arts, which also has a pair of Dale Chihuly art-glass installations. There is an excellent museum shop.

HISTORY MUSEUMS & HISTORIC LANDMARKS

Arizona Historical Society Museum in Papago Park. 1300 N. College Ave. (just off Curry Rd.), Tempe. ☎ **480/929-0292.** Free admission. Mon–Sat 10am–4pm; Sun noon–4pm. Bus: 66.

This museum, at the headquarters of the Arizona Historical Society, focuses its modern, well-designed exhibits on the history of central Arizona over the past century. Temporary exhibits on the lives and works of the people who helped shape this region are always highlights of a visit here. One of the more interesting permanent exhibits features life-size statues of everyday people from Arizona's past (a Mexican miner, a Chinese laborer, and so on). Quotes relate their individual stories, and props reveal what items they might have traveled with during their days in the desert.

✪ **Arizona State Capitol Museum.** 1700 W. Washington St. ☎ **602/542-4581.** Free admission. Mon–Fri 8am–5pm; Sat 10am–3pm. Closed state holidays. Bus: Yellow (Y).

In the years before Arizona became a state, the territorial capital moved from Prescott to Tucson, then back to Prescott, and finally settled in Phoenix. In 1898, a stately territorial capitol building was erected (with a copper roof to remind the local citizenry of the importance of that metal in the Arizona economy). Atop this copper roof was placed the statue *Winged Victory,* which still graces the old capitol building today. This building no longer serves as the actual state capitol, but has been restored to the way it appeared in 1912, the year Arizona became a state. Among the rooms on view are the senate and house chambers, as well as the governor's office. Excellent historical exhibits provide interesting perspectives on early Arizona events and lifestyles.

Historic Heritage Square. 115 N. 6th St., at Monroe. ☎ **602/262-5029** or 602/262-5071. Rosson House tours, $4 adults, $3 seniors, $1 children 6–12, free for children under 6. Hours vary for each building; call for information. Bus: Red (R), Yellow (Y), 0.

Although the city of Phoenix was founded as recently as 1870, much of its history has been obliterated. Heritage Square is a collection of some of the few remaining houses in Phoenix that date from the 19th century and the original Phoenix town site. All the buildings are listed on the National Register of Historic Places, and most display Victorian architectural styles popular just before the turn of the century. Today they house museums, restaurants, and gift shops. The Eastlake Victorian Rosson House, furnished with period antiques, is open for tours. The Silva House, a neoclassical revival-style home, houses historical exhibits on turn-of-the-century life in the Valley of the Sun. In the Stevens-Haustgen House, you'll find a gift shop, and in the Stevens House is the Arizona Doll and Toy Museum. The Burgess Carriage House contains a gift shop and ticket window for the Rosson House tours. The Teeter House, an 1899 bungalow, is a Victorian tearoom. The old Baird Machine Shop contains Pizzeria Bianco.

Phoenix Museum of History. 105 N. 6th St. ☎ **602/253-2734.** Admission $5 adults; $3.50 seniors, accommodations, and students; $2.50 children 6–12; free for children under 6. Mon–Sat 10am–5pm; Sun noon–5pm. Closed major holidays. Bus: Red (R) or Yellow (Y).

Located adjacent to Heritage Square in downtown Phoenix, this state-of-the-art museum is one of the anchors of the city's downtown revitalization plan. It presents an interesting look at the history of a city that, to the casual visitor, might not seem to *have* any history. Interactive exhibits get visitors involved in the displays, and unusual exhibits make this place much more interesting than your average local history museum. A beer-bottle sidewalk shows how one saloon-keeper solved the problem of the muddy streets that once plagued the city; another exhibit shows how "lungers" (tuberculosis sufferers) inadvertently helped originate the tourism industry in Arizona.

SCIENCE & INDUSTRY MUSEUMS

✪ **Arizona Science Center.** 600 E. Washington St. ☎ **602/716-2000.** www.azscience.org. Admission $8 adults, $6 seniors and children 3–12, free for children under 4. Planetarium and film combination tickets also available. Daily 10am–5pm. Closed Thanksgiving and Christmas. Bus: Red (R), Yellow (Y), 0.

Aimed primarily at children but also loads of fun for adults, the Arizona Science Center, a hands-on facility, is one of the anchors of Phoenix's ongoing renewal of the city's downtown. In this large facility you'll find state-of-the-art interactive exhibits covering a variety of topics from the human body to

Did You Know?

- Phoenix is the sixth-largest metropolitan area in the United States.
- The Phoenix area has more than 180 golf courses and more than 1,000 tennis courts.
- Some of the canals that water the Valley of the Sun were dug by hand by Native Americans hundreds of years ago.
- Each year Phoenix enjoys sunshine during 86% of all daylight hours, for a total of 300 to 315 sunny days.
- The tallest water fountain in the world (560 feet) is in the community of Fountain Hills east of Scottsdale.

coping with living in the desert. However, it is not the topics so much as the individual displays that make this museum fun. There's a huge ant farm, a virtual reality game that puts you inside a video game, a massive truck tire weighing almost 4 tons, a flight simulator, and a cloud maker. The ever-popular soap-bubble play area is housed on a terrace on the museum's roof, as is a stargazing area. In addition to the many exhibits, the science center includes a planetarium (night sky and laser shows) and a large-screen theater, both of which carry additional charges. There are also plenty of fun temporary exhibits.

Mesa Southwest Museum. 53 N. MacDonald St. (at the corner of 1st St.), Mesa. ☎ **480/644-2230.** Admission $4 adults, $3.50 seniors, $2 children 3–12, free for children under 3. Tues–Sat 10am–5pm; Sun 1–5pm. Closed major holidays. Bus: Red (R).

Located in downtown Mesa, this museum appeals mostly to children, but its exhibits on prehistoric indigenous cultures in the region will likely interest adults as well. Exhibits cover Mesoamerican art and Spanish mission life. Kids will love the fossils (including a complete mammoth skeleton) and animated dinosaurs. The mine and jail (this really was the old jail) displays are also a lot of fun for kids. There are usually a couple of different temporary exhibits at any given time that may include displays of contemporary art or regional history. The museum has recently expanded and in 2000 doubled its display space.

The museum also operates the nearby **Sirrine House Historic Home Museum,** 160 N. Center St., which is filled with period antiques from the late 19th and early 20th centuries. This historic home is open on weekends during the winter.

A MUSEUM MISCELLANY: PLANES, FLAMES & MORE

Arizona Mining & Mineral Museum. 1502 W. Washington St. ☎ **602/255-3795.** Free admission. Mon–Fri 8am–5pm; Sat 11am–4pm. Closed state holidays. Bus: Yellow (Y).

Arizonans have been romancing the stones for more than a century at colorfully named mines, such as the Copper Queen, the Sleeping Beauty, the No-Name Creek, the Lucky Boy, and the Bluebird. Out of such mines have come countless tons of copper, silver, and gold, as well as beautiful minerals with tongue-twisting names. Azurite, chalcanthite, chalcoaluminate, malachite, and chrysocolla are just some of the richly colored and fascinatingly textured minerals on display at this small downtown museum dedicated to the state's mining industry. Rather than playing up the historical or profit-making side of the industry, exhibits focus on the amazing variety and beauty of Arizona minerals.

Buffalo Museum of America. 10261 N. Scottsdale Rd. (at the southeast corner of Shea Blvd.), Scottsdale. ☎ **480/951-1022.** Admission $3 adults, $2.50 seniors, $2 children 6–17, free for children under 6. Mon–Fri 9am–5pm. Closed major holidays. Bus: 72 or 106.

Scottsdale may not be the home where the buffalo roam, but it does have a fascination with the Old West, so it seems appropriate to find here a museum dedicated to these fabled behemoths of the plains. This small museum is the culmination of one man's infatuation with the American bison, which is commonly known as the buffalo. The museum houses stuffed buffaloes, bronze buffaloes, buffalo paintings, and all manner of buffalo memorabilia, including a rifle that once belonged to Buffalo Bill Cody.

Champlin Fighter Aircraft Museum. 4636 Fighter Aces Dr., Mesa (at Falcon Field Airport off McKellips Rd.). ☎ **480/830-4540.** Admission $6.50 adults, $3 children 5–12, free for children under 5. Daily 10am–5pm. From U.S. 60, take the Greenfield exit, go north to McKellips Blvd., and follow the green signs.

This aeronautical museum, dedicated exclusively to fighter planes and the fighter aces who flew them, houses aircraft from World Wars I and II, the Korean War, and the Vietnam War, with a strong emphasis on the wood-and-fabric biplanes and triplanes of World War I (several Sopwiths and Fokkers). From World War II, there's a Spitfire, a Messerschmitt, and a Goodyear Corsair. Jet fighters from more recent battles include a MiG-15, a MiG-17, and an F4 Phantom. In total, there are 33 flyable fighters here.

Hall of Flame Firefighting Museum. Papago Park, 6101 E. Van Buren St. ☎ **602/275-3473.** Admission $5 adults, $4 seniors, $3 students 6–17, $1.50 children 3–5, free for children under 3. Mon–Sat 9am–5pm; Sun noon–4pm. Closed Jan 1, Thanksgiving, and Dec 25. Bus: 3.

The world's largest firefighting museum houses a fascinating collection of vintage fire trucks. The displays date from a 1725 English hand pumper to several classic fire engines from this century. All are beautifully restored and, of course, painted fire-engine red (mostly). In all, there are more than 90 vehicles on display.

3 Architectural Highlights

In addition to the architectural landmarks listed below, there are a couple of other buildings of which Phoenix is justly proud.

The **Arizona Biltmore,** 24th Street and Missouri Avenue (☎ **602/955-6600**), although not designed by Frank Lloyd Wright, shows the famed architect's hand in its distinctive cast-cement blocks and also displays sculptures, furniture, and stained glass designed by Wright. The best way to soak up the ambience of this exclusive resort (if you aren't staying here) is over dinner, cocktails, or tea. If you'd like to spend the day by the pool, you can even rent a cabana.

On a hilltop adjacent to the Arizona Biltmore, you can see the famed **Wrigley Mansion,** 2501 E. Telawa Trail (☎ **602/955-4079**), a classically elegant mansion that was built by chewing-gum magnate William Wrigley Jr. between 1929 and 1931 as a present for his wife, Ada. Built with Italianate styling, the many levels and red-tile roofs make it seem like an entire village. Today, the mansion is a National Historic Landmark with the interior restored to its original elegance. Tours are offered Tuesday and Thursday at 10am and 3pm and cost $10. Although this is currently a private 2club, lunch is open to the public.

Tovrea Castle, 5041 E. Van Buren St. (☎ **602/262-6412**), another architectural confection of the Phoenix landscape, has been likened to a giant wedding cake and is currently under renovation. However, it is scheduled to open to the public some time in mid-2001. Call for information.

Among the more recent buildings to garner architectural praise in Phoenix are the **new City Hall** and restored **Orpheum Theatre,** which sit back to back on Third Avenue between Washington and Adams streets. The new City Hall is a bold contemporary construction as intriguing as the main library, while the Orpheum is a classically elegant historic building. The two styles clash in a manner that typifies old and new Phoenix.

Opened in 1995, the **Burton Barr Library,** 1221 N. Central Ave. (☎ **602/262-4636**), is among the most daring pieces of public architecture in the city. No fan of futuristic art or science fiction should miss a visit. The five-story cube is partially clad in ribbed copper sheeting, enough copper to produce roughly 17,500,000 pennies (it took a lot of overdue books to pay for that feature). The building's design makes use of the desert's plentiful sunshine to provide light for reading, but also incorporates computer-controlled louvers and shade sails to reduce heat and glare.

Cosanti. 6433 Doubletree Ranch Rd., Scottsdale. Drive 1 mile west of Scottsdale Rd. on Doubletree Ranch Rd. ☎ **480/948-6145.** www.cosanti.com. Admission by donation; guided tours: minimum 5 people, $5 per person. Daily 9am–5pm. Closed major holidays.

This complex of cast-concrete structures served as a prototype and learning project for architect Paolo Soleri's much grander Arcosanti project currently under construction north of Phoenix (see "En Route to Northern Arizona" in chapter 8 for details). It's here at Cosanti that Soleri's famous bells are cast, and most weekday mornings, you can see the foundry in action.

Mystery Castle. 800 E. Mineral Rd. Take Central Ave. south to Mineral Rd. (2 miles south of Baseline Rd.) and turn east. ☎ **602/268-1581.** Admission $5 adults, $4 seniors, $2 children 5–14. Thurs–Sun 11am–4pm. Closed July–Sept.

Built for a daughter who longed for a castle more permanent than those built in sand at the beach, Mystery Castle is a wondrous work of folk-art architecture. Boyce Luther Gulley, who had come to Arizona in hopes of curing his tuberculosis, constructed the castle during the 1930s and early 1940s using stones from the property. The resulting 18-room fantasy has 13 fireplaces, a wedding chapel, parapets, and many other unusual touches. This castle is a must for fans of folk-art constructions, and tours are usually led by the daughter for whom the castle was built.

✪ **Taliesin West.** 12621 Frank Lloyd Wright Blvd. (at 114th St.), Scottsdale. ☎ **480/860-2700.** Basic tours, Oct 1–May 31 $14.50 adults, $12 seniors and students, $3 children 4–12, free for children 3 and under; June 1–Sept 30 $10 adults, $8 students and seniors, $3 children 4–12, free for children 3 and under. Oct 1–May 31 daily 10am–4pm; June 1–Sept 30 daily 8am–3pm. Closed Easter, Thanksgiving, Christmas, New Year's Day, and occasional special events. From Scottsdale Rd., go east on Shea Blvd. to 114th St., then north 1 mile to the entrance road.

Architect Frank Lloyd Wright fell in love with the Arizona desert and in 1937, opened a winter camp here that served as his office and school. Today, Taliesin West is the headquarters of the Frank Lloyd Wright Foundation and School of Architecture.

Tours explain the buildings of this campus and include a general background introduction to Wright and his theories of architecture. Wright believed in using local materials in his designs, and this shows up at Taliesin West where local stone was used for building foundations. He developed a number of innovative methods for dealing with the extremes of the desert climate, such as sliding wall panels to let in varying amounts of air and light.

Architecture students, and anyone interested in the work of Wright, will enjoy browsing through the excellent books in the gift shop. Expanded basic tours called Insight Tours ($20 adults, $16 seniors, students, and children), behind-the-scenes tours ($35 per person), and guided desert hikes ($20 per person) are also available at certain times of year. Call ahead and check the schedule to be sure you can get the tour you want at the time you want.

4 Zoos & Parks

The newest and perhaps most unusual park in the Phoenix metro area centers on the new **Tempe Town Lake,** created in 1999 by damming the Salt River with inflatable dams. With the construction of Tempe Town Lake, Tempe now has a

2-mile-long lake on which to go boating, and lining the north and south shores of the lake are bike paths and parks. The best lake access is at Tempe Town Beach, at the foot of the Mill Avenue Bridge. Here you can rent kayaks ($11.25 to $16.50 per hour) and other small boats. Tempe Town Lake is the focus of a grand development plan known as the Rio Salado Project, which will eventually include a hotel and other commercial facilities.

Among the city's most popular parks are its natural areas and preserves. These include South Mountain Park, Papago Park, Phoenix Mountains Preserve (site of Squaw Peak), North Mountain Preserve, North Mountain Recreation Area, and Camelback Mountain–Echo Canyon Recreation Area. For more information on these parks, see "Hiking," "Bicycling," and "Horseback Riding" under "Outdoor Pursuits," later in this chapter.

Out of Africa Wildlife Park. Fort McDowell Rd., Fountain Springs. ☎ **480/837-7779.** Admission $13.95 adults, $12.95 seniors, $4.95 children ages 3–12, free for children under 3. Oct 1–Memorial Day Tues–Sun 9:30am–5pm; Memorial Day–Sept Wed–Fri 4–9:30pm, Sat 9:30am–9:30pm, Sun 9:30am–5pm. Take Ariz. 87 northeast from Mesa and 2 miles past Shea Blvd., turn right on Fort McDowell Rd.

Lions and tigers and bears, oh my! That's what you'll see at this small wildlife park northeast of Scottsdale, and all these animals will be putting on shows for you rather than just lazing in the shade as they do at most zoos. The most popular performances are those in the park's swimming pool. You've probably never seen tigers, wolves, and bears having so much fun in the water.

The Phoenix Zoo. Papago Park, 455 N. Galvin Pkwy. ☎ **602/273-1341.** www.phoenixzoo.org. Admission $8.50 adults, $7.50 seniors, $4.25 children 3–12, free for children under 3. Labor Day–Apr daily 9am–5pm; May 1–Labor Day daily 7:30am–4pm. Closed Dec 25. Bus: 3.

Home to more than 1,300 animals, the Phoenix Zoo is known for its mixed-species, 4-acre African veldt exhibit and its baboon colony. The Southwestern animal exhibits are also of particular interest, as are the giant Galapagos tortoises. All the animals in the zoo are kept in naturalistic enclosures and what with all the palm trees and tropical vegetation, it's easy to forget that this is the desert, especially when you wander through the rainforest exhibit. Kids will enjoy Harmony Farm, a hands-on farm area.

5 Especially for Kids

In addition to the children's activities suggested below, kids are also likely to enjoy the Arizona Science Center, the Mesa Southwest Museum, the Hall of Flame Firefighting Museum, the Phoenix Zoo, and Out of Africa Wildlife Park—all described in detail above.

Arizona Doll & Toy Museum. In Heritage Square, 602 E. Adams St. ☎ **602/253-9337.** Admission $2.50 adults, $1 children. Tues–Sat 10am–4pm; Sun noon–4pm. Closed Aug. Bus: Red (R), Yellow (Y), 0.

Located in the Stevens House on Heritage Square in downtown Phoenix, the Arizona Doll and Toy Museum is as interesting to adults as it is to kids. "Class E. Dresser Ladies Shop" and "Hattie's Millinery and Dry Goods" miniature shop from the Mott Collection (which were originally at Knotts Berry Farm in Los Angeles) are on display.

Arizona Museum for Youth. 35 N. Robson St. (between Main and 1st sts.), Mesa. ☎ **480/644-2467.** www.ci.mesa.az.us/amfy. Admission $2.50, free for children under 2. Fall–spring Sun and Tues–Fri 1–5pm, Sat 10am–5pm; summer Tues–Sat 9am–5pm, Sun 1–5pm. Closed for 2 weeks between exhibits. Bus: R.

Using both traditional displays and participatory activities, this museum allows children to explore the fine arts and their own creativity. The museum is housed in a refurbished grocery store, which has for past exhibits been transformed into a zoo, a ranch, and a foreign country. Exhibits are geared mainly to toddlers through 12-year-olds, but all ages can work together to make an object or experience the activities.

Castles & Coasters. 9445 N. Metro Pkwy. E. ☎ **602/997-7575.** Ride and game prices vary. Open daily (hours change seasonally; call ahead). Bus: Red (R) or 27.

Located adjacent to Metrocenter, one of Arizona's largest shopping malls, this small amusement park boasts a very impressive rollercoaster and plenty of tamer rides. There are also four 18-hole miniature-golf courses and a huge pavilion full of video games.

CrackerJax Family Fun & Sports Park. 16001 N. Scottsdale Rd. (¼ mile south of Bell Rd.), Scottsdale. ☎ **480/998-2800.** Activity prices vary. Open daily (hours change seasonally; call ahead). Bus: 72.

Three miniature-golf courses are the main attraction here, but you'll also find a bilevel driving range, batting cages, go-cart tracks, sand volleyball courts, and a video-game arcade.

McCormick-Stillman Railroad Park. 7301 E. Indian Bend Rd., Scottsdale. ☎ **480/312-2312.** Train and carousel rides $1, train museum $1 ages 13 and up. Hours vary with the season, call for schedule. Bus: 72.

If you or your kids happen to like trains, then you won't want to miss this Scottsdale park dedicated to railroading. Within the park are a 5/12-scale model railroad that takes visitors around the park, restored cars and engines, two old railway depots, and model railroad layouts operated by a local club. There's also a 1929 carousel and a general store. You'll find the park on the corner of Scottsdale Road and Indian Bend Road.

6 Organized Tours & Excursions

The Valley of the Sun is a sprawling, often congested, place, and if you are unfamiliar with the area, you may be surprised at how great the distances are. If map reading and urban navigation are not your strong points, you may want to consider taking a guided tour. There are numerous companies offering tours of the Valley of the Sun; however, these tours tend to include only brief stops at highlights.

BUS TOURS **Gray Line of Phoenix** (☎ **800/732-0327** or 602/495-9100) is one of the largest tour companies in the valley. It offers a 3½-hour tour of Phoenix and the Valley of the Sun for $30 per adult. The tour points out such local landmarks as the state capitol, Heritage Square, Arizona State University, and Old Town Scottsdale.

GLIDER RIDES The thermals that form above the mountains in the Phoenix area are ideal for sailplane (glider) soaring. On the south side of the valley, **Arizona Soaring** (☎ **800/861-2318** in Arizona or 520/568-2318; 480/821-2903 for information), in the community of Maricopa, offers sailplane rides as well as instruction. A basic 20-minute flight is $69.95, and for $99.95 you can take an aerobatic flight with loops, rolls, and inverted flying. To reach the airstrip, take I-10 east to exit 164 (Maricopa Road), go 15 miles, turn west on Arizona 238 and continue for 6½ miles more. On the north side of the valley, there's **Turf Soaring School,** 8700 W. Carefree Hwy., Peoria (☎ **602/439-3621**), which charges $75 for a basic flight and $110 for an aerobatic flight. This outfit also offers flights for two people ($125), although your combined weight can't exceed 300 pounds.

Vacationing in the Fast Lane

Want to learn how to drive like a grand-prix racer? At the **Bob Bondurant School of High Performance Driving** (☎ **800/842-7223** or 520/796-1111; www.bondurant.com), you can do just that. For more than 30 years this school has been training drivers in how to handle cars the way the pros do. A 2½-hour Lap the Oval course (offered only twice a year) will run you $325 to $350, while a 4-day Grand Prix road racing course will set you back $3,275. Make reservations at least 3 months in advance.

HOT-AIR BALLOON RIDES The still morning air of the Valley of the Sun is perfect for hot-air ballooning, and because of the stiff competition, prices are among the lowest in the country—between $90 and $140 per person for a 1- to 1½-hour ride. Companies to try include **A Aerozona Adventure** (☎ **888/991-4260** or 480/991-4260), **Adventures Out West** (☎ **800/755-0935** or 602/996-6100), and **Unicorn Balloon Company** (☎ **800/468-2478** or 480/991-3666; www.unicornballoon.com).

JEEP TOURS Want to get off the pavement and do a little four-wheeling? Jeep tours through the desert are offered by a dozen or more companies around the valley. Most hotels and resorts have particular companies they work with, so if you want to do a Jeep tour, try contacting the concierge at your hotel. Alternatively, you can contact one of the following companies. Most will pick you up at your hotel, take you off through the desert, give you lots of information on this corner of the West, and maybe even let you try shooting a six-gun while you're out in the desert. Tour prices are around $65 to $100 for a 4-hour tour. Companies to try include **Western Events** (☎ **800/567-3619** or 480/860-1777), **Arizona Bound Tours** (☎ **480/994-0580**), and **Rawhide Land & Cattle** (☎ **800/294-JEEP** or 480/488-0023). The last company operates out of the popular Rawhide Wild West town/restaurant. For slightly more unique tours, try **Desert Storm Hummer Tours** (☎ **480/922-0020**), which uses those ultimate sport utility vehicles, or **Arizona Unique Buggy Adventures** (☎ **480/488-2466**), which uses unusual open-sided off-road buggies for its tours.

Some Jeep tour companies also offer the chance to do some gold panning. If this interests you, contact **Western Events** (☎ **800/567-3619** or 480/860-1777), which also does ghost-town excursions, or **Arrowhead Desert Tours** (☎ **800/514-9063** or 602/942-3361).

SCENIC FLIGHTS If you're short on time but still want to at least see the Grand Canyon, you can book an air tour in a small plane. **Westwind Tours** (☎ **888/869-0866** or 480/991-5557) charges $240 to $295 for its Grand Canyon tours and offers a trip for $415 that takes in Monument Valley as well. This company flies out of both the Scottsdale Airport and the Deer Valley Airport in the northwest part of the valley.

7 Outdoor Pursuits

BICYCLING Although the Valley of the Sun is a sprawling place, it's mostly flat, which makes bicycling a breeze as long as it isn't windy or in the heat of summer. **Wheels 'n Gear,** 7607 E. McDowell Rd., Scottsdale (☎ **480/945-2881**), in the Plaza Del Rio Shopping Center, rents mountain bikes for between $24 and $40 per day and has off-road trail maps available. Among the best mountain-biking spots in the city are South Mountain Park (use the entrance off 48th Street), Papago Park (at Van Buren Street and Galvin Parkway), and North Mountain Recreation Area (off Seventh Street between Dunlap Avenue and Thunderbird Road).

If you'd rather have someone show you some of the desert's best mountain biking, contact **Desert Biking Adventures** (☎ **888/249-BIKE** or 602/320-4602), which leads 2-, 3-, and 4-hour mountain-bike tours through the desert (and specializes in downhill rides). Tour prices range from $55 to $100.

If you'd rather confine your cycling to a paved surface, there's no better route than Scottsdale's **Indian Bend Wash greenbelt,** a paved multiuse path that extends for more than 15 miles along Hayden Road (from north of Shea Boulevard to Tempe). The Indian Bend Wash pathway can be accessed at many points along Hayden Road.

GOLF With nearly 200 courses in the Valley of the Sun, golf is just about the most popular sport in Phoenix and one of the main reasons people flock here during the winter months. Sunshine, spectacular views, and coyotes, quail, and doves for company make playing a round of golf in the valley a truly memorable experience.

However, despite the number of courses, it can still be difficult to get a tee time on any of the more popular courses (especially during the busy months of February through April). If you are staying at a resort with a golf course, be sure to make your tee-time reservations at the same time you make your room reservations. If you aren't staying at a resort, you might still be able to play a round on a resort course if you can get a last-minute tee time. Try one of the tee-time reservation services below.

The only thing harder than getting a winter or spring tee time in the Valley of the Sun is facing the bill at the end of your 18 holes. Greens fees at most public and resort courses range from around $90 to $125, with the top courses at the most expensive resorts often charging around $180 (or even more). Municipal courses, on the other hand, charge less than $30. You can save money on many courses by opting for twilight play, which usually begins at 1, 2, or 3pm. We've listed high- and low-season greens fees below; you'll find that spring and fall fees fall somewhere in-between.

You can get more information on Valley of the Sun golf courses from the **Greater Phoenix Convention & Visitors Bureau,** 50 N. Second St., Phoenix, AZ 85004 (☎ **877/225-5749** or 602/254-6500). You can also pick up a copy of the *Greater Phoenix Golf Guide* at the Visitors Bureau, golf courses, and many hotels and resorts.

To make sure you get to play those courses you've been dreaming about, it's a good idea to make reservations well in advance. Many companies around the valley will save you the hassle of booking tee times by making reservations for you. One of these companies, **Golf Xpress** (☎ **800/878-8580** or 602/404-GOLF), can make reservations farther in advance than you could if you called the golf course direct. This company also makes hotel reservations, rents golf clubs, and provides other assistance to golfers visiting the valley. **Par-Tee-Time Golf** (☎ **800/827-2223** or 602/230-7223) is another company that makes advance reservations. For last-minute reservations, call **Stand-by Golf** (☎ **480/874-3133**).

The valley's many resort courses are, of course, the favored fairways of valley visitors. For spectacular scenery, the two Jay

Morrish–designed 18-hole courses at ✪ **The Boulders,** 34631 N. Tom Darlington Dr., Carefree (☎ **800/553-1717** or 480/488-9028), just can't be beat. Given the option, play the South Course and watch out as you approach the tee box on the seventh hole—it's a real heart stopper. Tee times for non-resort guests are very limited in the winter and spring, and you'll pay $225 for a round. However, in summer you can play here for only $75 (just be sure you get the earliest possible tee time and bring plenty of water).

Jumping over to Litchfield Park, on the far west side of the valley, you'll find **The Wigwam Golf and Country Club,** 300 Wigwam Blvd. (☎ **623/935-3811**), and, count 'em, three championship 18-hole courses. ✪ **The Gold Course** here is legendary, but even the Blue and Red courses are worth playing. These are traditional courses for purists who want vast expanses of green instead of cactus and boulders. In the high season, greens fees are $130 for the Gold Course and $100 ($55 twilight) for the Blue and Red courses (in summer, $38). High-season reservations for non-guests can be made no more than 5 days in advance.

Way over on the east side of the valley at the foot of the Superstition Mountains is the ✪ **Gold Canyon Golf Resort,** 6100 S. Kings Ranch Rd., Gold Canyon (☎ **480/982-9449**), which has been rated one of the best public courses in the state and has what have been rated as three of the best holes in the state—the second, third, and fourth holes on the Dinosaur Mountain course, a visually breathtaking desert-style course. Greens fees on this course range from $95 to $110 in winter and $50 to $60 in summer. The resort's second course, the Sidewinder, is a more traditional course and is less dramatic, but is much more economical. Greens fees in winter range from $45 to $65 and from $35 to $55 in summer. Make reservations a week in advance. It's well worth the drive.

If you want to swing where the pros do, beg, borrow, or steal a tee time on the Tom Weiskopf and Jay Morrish–designed Stadium Course at the ✪ **Tournament Players Club (TPC) of Scottsdale,** 17020 N. Hayden Rd. (☎ **480/585-3600** or 480/585-3939), which annually hosts the Phoenix Open. The 18th hole here has standing room for 40,000 spectators, but it is hoped there won't be that many around (or any TV cameras) the day you double-bogey on this hole. The TPC's second 18, the Desert Course, is actually a municipal course, thanks to an agreement with the landowner, the Bureau of Land Management. Stadium course greens fees are $181 in the winter/spring and $81 in the summer. Desert Course greens fees range from $38 to $48.

At the **Gainey Ranch Golf Club,** at the Hyatt Regency Scottsdale Resort at Gainey Ranch, 7600 E. Gainey Club Dr. (☎ **480/951-0022**), you'll find three decidedly different 9-hole courses (the Dunes, the Arroyo, and the Lakes courses), each with its own set of challenges. However, these courses are open only to guests of the resort.

If a traditional course that has been played by presidents and celebrities alike interests you, then try to get a tee time at one of the two 18-hole courses at the **Arizona Biltmore Country Club,** 24th Street and Missouri Avenue (☎ **602/955-9655**). The two courses here are more relaxing than challenging, good to play if you're not yet up to par. Greens fees are $150 in the winter/spring and $48 in summer. Reservations can be made 30 days in advance. There's also a championship 18-hole putting course at the hotel.

The two courses at the **Camelback Golf Club,** 7847 N. Mockingbird Lane (☎ **480/596-7050**), offer distinctly different experiences. However, the Resort course has recently undergone a complete redesign, with new water features, among other changes. The Indian Bend course is a links-style course with great mountain views and lots of water hazards. Greens fees are $105 to $185 in winter/spring and $30 to $75 in summer. Make reservations up to 30 days in advance.

Set at the base of Camelback Mountain, **The Phoenician Golf Club,** 6000 E. Camelback Rd. (☎ **800/888-8234** or 480/423-2449), at the valley's most glamorous resort, has 27 holes that mix traditional and desert styles. Greens fees if you aren't staying at the resort are $180 in winter/spring and $90 in summer.

Of the valley's many daily-fee courses, it is the two 18-hole courses at ✪ **Troon North Golf Club,** 10320 E. Dynamite Blvd., Scottsdale (☎ **480/585-5300**), seemingly just barely carved out of raw desert, that garner the most local accolades. Greens fees are $240 in winter/spring and $75 to $90 through the summer. Reservations are taken up to 30 days in advance (and fill up quickly in winter).

However, the Pete Dye–designed **ASU-Karsten Golf Course,** 1125 E. Rio Salado Pkwy., Tempe (☎ **480/921-8070**), part of Arizona State University, is also highly praised and a very challenging training ground for top collegiate golfers. Greens fees are $65 to $88 in the winter and $25 in the summer. Make reservations at least 5 days in advance in the winter.

If you haven't yet gotten your handicap down, but want to try a desert-style course, then head to **Tatum Ranch Golf Club,** 29888 N. Tatum Ranch Dr., Cave Creek (☎ **480/585-2399**), which is regarded as a forgiving course with a desert sensibility. However, this course is in the process of going private and may no longer be accepting outside players by the time you read this. Greens fees are $60 to $110 in the winter and somewhere around $40 to $60 in the summer.

Other worthwhile daily-fee courses include **Kokopelli Golf Resort,** 1800 W. Guadelupe Rd., Gilbert (☎ **480/926-3589** or 480/962-GOLF), with greens fees of $75 in winter and $39 in summer, and **The Legend at Arrowhead,** 21027 N. 67th Ave., Glendale (☎ **623/561-1902** or 480/962-GOLF), with greens fees of $60 to $80 in winter and $25 to $35 in summer. The **Kierland Golf Club,** 15636 Clubgate Dr., Scottsdale (☎ **480/922-9283**), which was designed by Scott Miller and consists of three 9-hole courses that can be played in combination, is another much-talked-about local daily-fee course. Greens fees are $125 to $145 in winter and $50 to $65 in summer.

Of the municipal courses in Phoenix, **Papago Golf Course,** 5595 E. Moreland St. (☎ **602/275-8428**), at the foot of the red sandstone Papago Buttes, offers fine views and economical rates ($18 to $28 in high season) and has a killer 17th hole. **Encanto Golf Course,** 2775 N. 15th Ave. (☎ **602/253-3963**), is equally inexpensive for a round of golf ($18 to $28 in the high season). Keep in mind that these rates don't include a golf cart, which is another $18 or so.

HIKING Several mountains around Phoenix, including Camelback Mountain and Squaw Peak, have been set aside as parks and nature preserves, and these natural areas are among the city's most popular hiking spots. The city's largest nature preserve, **Phoenix South Mountain Park,** said to be the largest city park in the world, contains miles of hiking, mountain-biking, and horseback-riding trails, and the views of Phoenix from here are spectacular, especially at sunset. To reach the park, simply drive south on Central Avenue or 48th Street.

Perhaps the most popular hiking trail in the city is the trail to the top of ✪ **Camelback Mountain,** which is near the boundary between Phoenix and Scottsdale. This is the highest mountain in Phoenix, and the 1.2-mile trail to the summit is very steep. Don't attempt this one in the heat of the day, and take at least a quart of water with you. The reward for your effort is the city's finest view. To reach the trailhead for Camelback Mountain, drive up 44th Street until it becomes McDonald Drive, then turn right on East Echo Canyon Drive, and continue up the hill until the road ends at a large parking lot.

At the east end of Camelback Mountain you'll find the Cholla Trail, which is longer than the trail at the west end and sees far fewer hikers. The only parking for this trail is along Invergordon Road at Chaparral Road, just north of Camelback Road (along the east boundary of The Phoenician resort). Be sure to park in a legal parking space and watch the hours that parking is allowed. This trail starts out fairly easy and then toward the top gets steep, rocky, and quite difficult. However, there are great views down onto the fairways of The Phoenician's golf course.

Squaw Peak in the Phoenix Mountains Preserve offers another aerobic workout of a hike and has views almost as spectacular as those from Camelback Mountain. Squaw Peak is reached from Squaw Peak Drive off Lincoln Drive between 22nd and 23rd streets.

For much less vigorous hiking, try the North Mountain Recreation Area in North Mountain Preserve. This natural area, located on either side of Seventh Street between Dunlap Avenue and Thunderbird Road, has more flat hiking than Camelback Mountain or Squaw Peak.

Farther afield are numerous hiking opportunities in the Superstition Mountains to the east and the McDowell Mountains to the north.

HORSEBACK RIDING Even in the urban confines of the Phoenix metro area, people like to play at being cowboys, and if you get the urge to saddle up, there are plenty of places around the valley to go for a horseback ride. Keep in mind that most stables require or prefer reservations.

On the south side of the city, try **Ponderosa Stables,** 10215 S. Central Ave. (☎ **602/268-1261**), or **South Mountain Stables,** 10005 S. Central Ave. (☎ **602/276-8131**), both of which lead rides into South Mountain Park and charge $17 per hour. In the Scottsdale area, try **MacDonald's Ranch,** 26540 N. Scottsdale Rd. (☎ **480/585-0239**), which charges $24 for a 1-hour ride and $36 for a 2-hour ride.

On the east side of the Valley, you'll find several riding stables in the foothills of the Superstition Mountains. **Trail Horse Adventures,** 2151 N. Warner Rd., Apache Junction (☎ **800/SADDLEUP** or 480/982-6353), which offers rides ranging in length from 2 hours to all day ($33 to $135) or longer. The company arranges riding lessons, overnight pack trips, picnics, and hayrides. Over in Gold Canyon, you'll find one of the most famous names in Arizona horseback riding. **Don Donnelly Stables,** 6010 Kings Ranch Rd., Gold Canyon (☎ **800/346-4403** or 480/982-7822), offers 2-hour sunset rides for $36 per person. These stables also do overnight rides, cookouts, and hayrides.

IN-LINE SKATING In the Scottsdale area, you can rent in-line skates, including all protective equipment, at **Scottsdale Bladez,** 14692 Frank Lloyd Wright Blvd. (☎ **480/391-1139**), for $4 per hour or $12 per day. You can also rent equipment at **Wheels 'n Gear,** 7607 E. McDowell Rd. (☎ **480/945-2881**), which is in the Plaza Del Rio Shopping Center (adjacent to the popular Indian Bend Wash greenbelt trail) and charges $6 for 2 hours or $12 per day.

The folks at these shops can point you toward nearby spots that are good for skating. One of the best places to skate is the **Indian Bend Wash greenbelt,** a paved multiuse path that extends for around 15 miles. It runs parallel to Hayden Road in Scottsdale from north of Shea Boulevard to Washington Street. The Indian Bend Wash pathway can be accessed at many points along Hayden Road.

TENNIS Most major hotels in the area have one or more tennis courts, and there are several tennis resorts around the valley. If you're staying someplace without a tennis court, try the **Scottsdale Ranch Park,** 10400 E. Via Linda, Scottsdale

(☎ **480/312-7774**). Court fees range from $3 to $5 for 1½ hours of singles play.

WATER PARKS At **Waterworld Safari Water Park,** 4243 W. Pinnacle Peak Rd., Glendale (☎ **623/581-1947**), you can free-fall 6½ stories down the Avalanche speed waterslide or catch a gnarly wave in the wave pool. Other waterslides offer tamer times. **Mesa Golfland-Sunsplash,** 155 W. Hampton, Mesa (☎ **480/834-8319**), has a wave pool and a tunnel called "the Black Hole." **Big Surf,** 1500 N. McClintock Rd. (☎ **480/947-7873**), has a wave pool, underground tube slides, and more.

All three of these parks charge about $16 for adults and $13 for children 4 to 11 (prices tend to go down after 3 or 4pm). All are open from approximately Memorial Day to Labor Day, Monday to Saturday 10am to about 8 or 9pm (Big Surf until 6pm only) and Sunday 11am to 7pm.

WHITE-WATER RAFTING & TUBING ON THE SALT RIVER The desert may not seem like the place for white-water rafting, but up in the mountains to the northeast of Phoenix, the ✪ **Upper Salt River** still flows wild and free and offers some exciting rafting. Most years from about late February to late May, snowmelt from the White Mountains turns the river into a Class III and IV river filled with exciting rapids (however, some years there just isn't enough water). Companies operating full-day, overnight, and multiday rafting trips on the upper Salt River (conditions permitting) include **Far Flung Adventures** (☎ **800/231-7238** or 520/425-7272; www.farflung.com), **Sun Country Rafting** (☎ **800/272-3353** or 602/493-9011), and **Mild to Wild Rafting** (☎ **800/567-6745**). Prices range from around $80 to $100 for a day trip up to around $650 for a multiday trip. Mild to Wild also offers 2- and 4-day float trips on the Verde River.

Tamer river trips can be had from **Salt River Recreation** (☎ **480/984-3305**), which has its headquarters 20 miles northeast of Phoenix on the Bush Highway (Power Road) at the intersection of Usery Pass Road in the Tonto National Forest. For $10, the company will rent you a large inner tube and shuttle you by bus upriver for the float down. The inner-tubing season runs from May through September.

8 Spectator Sports

Phoenix has gone nuts over pro sports and is now one of the few cities in the country with all four of the major sports teams (baseball, basketball, football, and hockey). Add to this baseball's spring training, a second ice hockey team, professional women's basketball, three major golf tournaments, the annual Fiesta Bowl college football classic, and ASU football, basketball, and baseball, and you have enough action to keep even the most rabid sports fans happy. For sports fans, the best month to visit is probably March, when you could feasibly catch spring baseball training, the Suns, the Coyotes, and ASU basketball and baseball, as well as the Franklin Templeton Tennis Classic, The Tradition, and the Standard Register PING LPGA Tournament.

Call **ETM/Dillard's Box Office** (☎ **800/638-4253** or 480/503-5555) or **Ticketmaster** (☎ **480/784-4444;** www.ticketmaster.com) for tickets to most of the events below. For tickets to sold-out events, try **Tickets Unlimited** (☎ **800/289-8497** or 602/840-2340) or **Ticket Exchange** (☎ **800/800-9811** or 602/254-4444).

AUTO RACING At the **Phoenix International Raceway,** 7602 S. 115th Ave. (at Baseline Road), Avondale (☎ **602/252-2227**), there is NASCAR and Indy car racing on the world's fastest 1-mile oval. Tickets range from $10 to $40.

BASEBALL The **Arizona Diamondbacks** (☎ **602/514-8400**) play in downtown Phoenix at the Bank One Ballpark (BOB), a state-of-the-art stadium with a retractable roof that allows for comfortable play during Phoenix's blistering summer temperatures. The retractable roof makes this one of the only enclosed baseball stadiums with natural grass. Tickets ($4 to $55) are available at the Bank One Ballpark ticket office and through ETM/Dillard's Box Office outlets (☎ **800/638-4253** or 480/503-5555; www.etm.com).

For decades, however, it has been spring training that has given Phoenix its annual shot of baseball, and don't think that the Cactus League's preseason exhibition games will be any less popular just because the Diamondbacks are in town. Spring-training games may rank second only to golf in popularity with winter visitors to the valley. Seven major league baseball teams have spring-training camps around the valley during March and April, and exhibition games are scheduled at six different stadiums. Ticket prices range from $3 to $19. Tickets for the Diamondbacks, Cubs, and Athletics are sold through ETM/Dillard's Box Office outlets (☎ **800/638-4253** or 480/503-5555), tickets for the Padres, Mariners, Brewers, and Angels are sold through Ticketmaster (☎ **480/784-4444**), and tickets for the Giants are sold through Bass Tickets (☎ **800/225-2277**). Get a schedule of games from the convention and visitors bureau or an ETM/Dillard's Box Office outlet, or check the *Arizona Republic* while you're in town. Games often sell out, especially on weekends, so be sure to order tickets in advance if you're a serious fan.

Teams training in the valley include the **San Francisco Giants,** Scottsdale Stadium, 7408 E. Osborn Rd., Scottsdale (☎ 800/225-2277 or 480/312-2580); the **Oakland A's,** Phoenix Municipal Stadium, 5999 E. Van Buren St., Phoenix (☎ 602/392-0217); the **Anaheim Angels,** Tempe Diablo Stadium, 2200 W. Alameda Dr., Tempe (☎ 480/438-9300); the **Chicago Cubs,** HoHoKam Park, 1235 N. Center St., Mesa (☎ 480/964-4467), the **San Diego Padres,** Peoria Sports Complex, 16101 N. 83rd Ave., Peoria (☎ 800/409-1511 or 623/878-4337), the **Seattle Mariners,** Peoria Sports Complex, 16101 N. 83rd Ave., Peoria (☎ 800/409-1511 or 623/878-4337), and the **Milwaukee Brewers,** Maryvale Baseball Park, 3508 N. 53rd Ave., Phoenix (☎ 623/245-5500).

BASKETBALL The NBA's **Phoenix Suns** play at the America West Arena, 201 E. Jefferson St. (☎ **602/379-SUNS**). Tickets are $10 to $80 and are available at the America West Arena box office and through ETM/Dillard's Box Office outlets (see above). Suns tickets are hard to come by. If you want good seats, you really have to buy your tickets on the day they go on sale (usually in mid-September). If you forget to plan ahead, try contacting the box office the day before or the day of a game to see if tickets have been returned. Otherwise, you'll have to try a ticket agency and pay the premium.

Phoenix also has a Women's National Basketball Association (WNBA) team, the **Phoenix Mercury** (☎ **602/252-WNBA** or 602/379-7800) that plays at the America West Arena, 201 E. Jefferson St., between mid-June and mid-August. Ticket prices range from $8 to $36.

FOOTBALL The **Arizona Cardinals** (☎ **800/999-1402** or 602/379-0102) play at Arizona State University's Sun Devil Stadium, which is also home to the Fiesta Bowl Football Classic. Tickets are $30 to $125. Except for a few specific games each season, it is generally possible to get Cardinals tickets.

While the Cardinals get to use Sun Devil Stadium, this field really belongs to Arizona State University's **Sun Devils** (☎ **480/965-2381**). Tickets are $16 and are sold through ETM/Dillard's Box Office outlets (see above).

Despite the desert heat and presence of a baseball team, Phoenicians don't give up football just because it's summer. The **Arizona Rattlers** arena football team (☎ **602/514-8383**) plays 50-yard indoor football at the America West Arena, 201 E. Jefferson St. Tickets are $9 to $37 and are available at the America West Arena box office.

GOLF TOURNAMENTS It's not surprising that, with nearly 200 golf courses and ideal golfing weather throughout the winter and spring, the Valley of the Sun hosts three major PGA tournaments each year. Tickets for all three tournaments are available through ETM/Dillard's Box Office outlets (see above).

The **Phoenix Open Golf Tournament** (☎ **602/870-0163;** www.phoenixopen.com) in January is the largest. Held at the Tournament Players Club (TPC) of Scottsdale, this tournament attracts more spectators than any other golf tournament in the world (nearly 400,000 each year). The 18th hole of the TPC has standing room for 40,000. Tickets usually go on sale in June with prices starting around $20.

Each March, the **Standard Register PING LPGA Tournament** (☎ **602/495-4653**), held in the year 2000 at the Legacy Golf Resort, lures nearly 150 of the top women golfers from around the world. Daily ticket prices are $15, and weekly tickets are around $50.

The Tradition (☎ **480/595-4070**), a Senior PGA Tour event held each April at the Desert Mountain golf course, has a loyal following of fans who would rather watch the likes of Jack Nicklaus and Lee Trevino than see Tiger Woods win yet another tournament. Daily tickets are $40, and they usually go on sale in January.

Now even amateurs can get in on some tournament action at the **Phoenix Amateur Golf Championship**

(☎ **877/988-GOLF**), which is held in mid-July (partly to prove that it's possible to play golf in the summer in Phoenix).

HOCKEY Ice hockey in the desert? It may not make sense, but even Phoenicians are crazy about ice hockey (maybe it's all those northern transplants). The NHL's **Phoenix Coyotes** (☎ **888/255-PUCK** or 480/563-PUCK) play at America West Arena, 201 E. Jefferson St. Tickets range from $10.50 to $80. Tickets are sold through ETM/Dillard's Box Office outlets (see above).

HORSE/GREYHOUND RACING The **Phoenix Greyhound Park,** 3801 E. Washington St. (☎ **602/273-7181**), is a large, fully enclosed, and air-conditioned facility offering seating in various grandstands, lounges, and restaurants. There's racing throughout the year, and tickets are $1.50 to $3.

Turf Paradise, 1501 W. Bell Rd. (☎ **602/942-1101**), is Phoenix's horse-racing track. The season runs from October to May, with post time at 12:30pm Friday through Tuesday. Admission ranges from $1 to $5.

RODEOS, POLO & HORSE SHOWS Cowboys, cowgirls, and other horsey types will find plenty of the four-legged critters going through their paces most weeks at **Westworld Equestrian Center,** 16601 N. Pima Rd., Scottsdale (☎ **480/312-6802**). With its 400 stalls, 11 equestrian arenas, and a polo field, this 400-acre complex provides an amazing variety of entertainment and sporting events. There are rodeos, polo matches, an Arabian horse show, horse rentals, and horseback-riding instruction. Ticket prices vary with the event.

TENNIS TOURNAMENTS Each March, top international men's tennis players compete at the **Franklin Templeton Tennis Classic** (☎ **480/922-0222**), which is held at the Scottsdale Princess Resort, 7575 E. Princess Dr., Scottsdale. Tickets run about $10 to $55 and are available through ETM/Dillard's Box Office outlets (see above).

9 Day Spas

Ever since the first "lungers" showed up in the Phoenix area hoping to cure their tuberculosis, the desert has been a magnet for those looking to get healthy. In the first half of the 20th century, health spas were all the rage in Phoenix, and with the health-and-fitness trend continuing to gather steam, it comes as no surprise that health spas are now immensely popular in the Valley of the Sun. In the past few years, several of the area's top resorts have added new full-service health spas or expanded existing ones to cater to guest's increasing requests for services such as massages, body wraps, mud masks, and salt glows.

If you can't or don't want to spend the money to stay at a top resort and avail yourself of the spa, you may still be able to indulge. Most of the valley's resorts open the doors of their spas to the public, and, for the cost of a body treatment or massage, you can spend the day at the spa, taking classes, working out in a fitness room, lounging by the pool, and otherwise living the life of the rich and famous. Barring this indulgence, you can slip into a day spa, of which there are many scattered around the valley, and take a stress-reduction break the way other people take a latte break.

The new hot and happening place to be pampered is ✪ **The Gainey Village Health Club and Spa,** 7477 E. Doubletree Ranch Rd., Scottsdale (☎ **480/609-6980**), a state-of-the-art spa and exercise facility near the Hyatt Regency Scottsdale resort. Specialized treatments include massage in a hydrotherapy tub or with water pressure and a couples massage (complete with champagne and chocolate truffles) in a VIP room with a waterfall shower. Of course, spa treatments include just about anything else you can think of, from mineral skin glows to pumpkin peels to purifying facials. With any hour-long treatment here (average price $75 to $95), you can use the extensive exercise facilities or take a class.

Located high on the flanks of Mummy Mountain with a nice view over the valley, **The Spa at Camelback Inn,** 5402 E. Lincoln Dr., Scottsdale (☎ **480/596-7020**), is a great place to spend the day being pampered. For the cost of a single 1-hour treatment—between $95 and $105—you can use all the facilities. Among the treatments available is a para-joba body moisturizer that will leave your skin feeling like silk. Multiple-treatment packages range in price from $150 to $275.

The **Centre for Well Being,** at The Phoenician, 6000 E. Camelback Rd., Scottsdale (☎ **800/843-2392** or 480/423-2452), is the valley's most prestigious day spa, the place to head if you want to be pampered with the rich and famous.

For anywhere from $95 to $355, you can spend the day at the spa receiving one or more treatments and using the spa's many facilities. A single treatment (say a thermal Moor mud wrap or a Turkish body scrub) entitles you to use the facilities for the rest of the day.

If you want a truly spectacular setting for your day at the spa, head north to Carefree and the **Sonoran Spa at The Boulders,** 34631 N. Tom Darlington Dr. (☎ **480/488-9009**). Here individual treatments cost $99 to $135, and day-packages run about $285. Included with any treatment is use of the extensive facilities and lap pool. At press time, there were plans to build a Golden Door health spa in 2001. When completed, this should become one of the valley's top spas.

The historic setting and convenient location of the **Arizona Biltmore Spa,** 24th Street and Missouri Avenue (☎ **800/950-0086** or 602/955-6600), make this 20,000-square-foot facility an excellent choice if you're spending time along the Camelback Corridor. The spa menu is extensive and includes the likes of balneotherapy, water goddess Sedona mud purification treatment, lymphatic massages, and bindi herbal body treatments. If you aren't staying at the resort, you can use the facilities for $25; body and beauty treatments range from $60 to $175. Use of the facilities is free with a 60-minute treatment.

The Mist Spa, at the Radisson Resort & Spa Scottsdale, 7171 N. Scottsdale Rd., Scottsdale (☎ **877/MIST-SPA** or 480/905-2882), allows non-resort guests use of the facilities for $25 per day (fee is waived with purchase of a 50-minute spa treatment). The 20,000-square-foot spa has a Japanese design, complete with Japanese-style massage rooms and a tranquil rock garden in a central covered courtyard. Spa treatments, which include the likes of collagen facials, honey steam wraps, Dead Sea mud wraps, and green tea detoxifying wraps, cost between $70 and $115.

10 Shopping

For the most part, shopping in the Valley of the Sun means malls. They're everywhere, and they're air-conditioned, which, we're sure you'll agree, makes shopping in the desert far more enjoyable when it's 110°F outside.

Scottsdale and the Biltmore District of Phoenix (along Camelback Road) are the valley's main upscale shopping areas, while Old Scottsdale (one of the few outdoor shopping areas) plays host to hundreds of boutiques, galleries, jewelry stores, and Native American crafts stores. The Western atmosphere of Old Scottsdale is partly real and partly a figment of the local merchants' imaginations, but nevertheless it's the most popular tourist shopping area in the valley. It also happens to be the heart of the valley's art market, with dozens of art galleries along Main Street.

Shopping hours are usually Monday through Saturday 10am to 6pm and Sunday noon to 5pm, and malls usually stay open until 9pm Monday to Saturday.

ANTIQUES

Downtown Glendale (located west of Phoenix) is the valley's main antiques district. Four times a year, the Phoenix Antique Market (☎ **800/678-9987** or 602/943-1766) stages Arizona's largest collectors' shows at the Arizona State Fairgrounds, 19th Avenue and McDowell Road. Call for dates.

Antiques Super-Mall. 1900 N. Scottsdale Rd., Scottsdale. ☎ **480/874-2900.**

If you make only one antiques stop, make it here. This is one of the biggest antiques malls in the valley and within a block are two others: the **Antique Centre,** 2012 N. Scottsdale Rd. (☎ **480/675-9500**), and the **Antique Trove,** 2020 N. Scottsdale Rd. (☎ **480/947-6074**).

Arizona West Galleries. 7149 E. Main St., Scottsdale. ☎ **480/994-3752.**

Nowhere else in Scottsdale will you find such an amazing collection of cowboy collectibles and Western antiques. There are antique saddles and chaps, old rifles and six-shooters, sheriff's badges, spurs, and the like.

Bishop Gallery for Art & Antiques. 7164 Main St., Scottsdale. ☎ **480/949-9062.**

This cramped shop is wonderfully eclectic, featuring everything from Asian antiques to unusual original art. Definitely worth a browse.

ART

In the Southwest, only Santa Fe is a more important art market than Scottsdale, and along the streets of Old Scottsdale you'll find dozens of ✪ **art galleries** selling everything from monumental bronzes to contemporary art created from found objects. On Main Street, you'll find primarily cowboy art, both traditional and contemporary, while on North Marshall Way, you'll find much more imaginative and daring contemporary art.

Art One. 4120 N. Marshall Way, Scottsdale. ☎ **480/946-5076.**

If you want to see the possible directions that area artists will be heading in the next few years, stop in at this Marshall Way gallery that specializes in works by art students and other area cutting-edge artists. The works here can be surprisingly good, and the prices are very reasonable.

gallerymateria. 4222 N. Marshall Way, Scottsdale. ☎ **480/949-1262.**

It's difficult to classify this fascinating boutique, which answers the question, "Is it useful, or is it art?" with clothing and household items that could double as art (with prices to match). You'll also find jewelry that looks like miniature sculptures, and crafts at the cutting edge of style using new materials or traditional materials in innovative ways. There are two parts to the boutique, and in between there's a sculpture courtyard.

✪ **Lisa Sette Gallery.** 4142 N. Marshall Way, Scottsdale. ☎ **480/990-7342.**

If you aren't a fan of cowboy or Native American art, you may feel left out of the Scottsdale art scene. Don't despair. Instead, drop by this gallery, which represents premier glass-artist William Morris as well as many others. International, national, and local artists share wall space here, with a wide mix of media represented.

Meyer Gallery. 7173 E. Main St., Scottsdale. ☎ **480/947-6372.**

This gallery is most notable for its selection of Old West, landscape, and mood paintings by living impressionists. The proprietor also has a cute Jack Russell terrier that likes to chase tennis balls.

Overland Gallery. 7155 Main St., Scottsdale. ☎ **480/947-1934.**

Traditional Western paintings and a collection of Russian Impressionist paintings form the backbone of this gallery's fine collection. These are museum-quality works (prices sometimes approach $100,000) and definitely worth a look.

Roberts Gallery. In El Pedregal Festival Marketplace, 34505 N. Scottsdale Rd., Carefree. ☎ **480/488-1088.**

The feathered masks and sculptures of Virgil Walker are the highlights at this gallery, and if you have an appreciation for fine detail work, you'll likely be fascinated by these pieces. Walker creates fantasy figures, every inch of which is covered with feathers.

BOOKS

Major chain bookstores in the Phoenix and Scottsdale area include **Borders Books Music & Café** at 2402 E. Camelback Rd., Phoenix (☎ **602/957-6660**), and **Barnes & Noble Booksellers** at 10235 N. Metro Parkway East, Phoenix (☎ **602/678-0088**), 4847 E. Ray Rd., Phoenix (☎ **480/940-7136**), and 10500 N. 90th St., Scottsdale (☎ **480/391-0048**).

T. A. Swinford. 7134 W. Main St., Scottsdale. ☎ **480/946-0022.**

Rare and out-of-print books about the American West are the specialty here. If you're looking for the likes of *Triggernometry, A Gallery of Gunfighters* (1934) or *Range Murder: How the Red-Sash Gang Dry-Gulched Deputy United States Marshal George Wellman* (1955), you'll find it here.

A CHOCOLATERIE

✪ **Chocolaterie Bernard C.** In Hilton Village, 6137 N. Scottsdale Rd. ☎ **480/483-3139.**

If you have *ever* had a genuine Belgian praline (chocolate, not one of those puffy cookies), then you will not want to leave Scottsdale without paying a visit to this chocolate shop. If you have *never* had a Belgian chocolate, you won't want to miss this shop either. The exquisite chocolate confections here will make you forget all about Godiva.

FASHION

WESTERN WEAR

Az-Tex Hat Company. 3903 N. Scottsdale Rd., Scottsdale. ☎ **800/972-2116** or 480/481-9900.

If you're looking to bring home a cowboy hat from your trip to Arizona, this is a good place to get it. The small shop in Old Scottsdale offers custom shaping and fitting of both felt and woven hats. There's a second store at 15044 N. Cave Creek Rd., Phoenix (☎ **602/971-9090**).

Out West. In El Pedregal Festival Marketplace, 34505 N. Scottsdale Rd., Carefree. ☎ **888/454-WEST** or 480/488-0180.

If the revival of 1950s cowboy fashions and interior decor has hit your nostalgia button, then you'll want to hightail it up to this eclectic shop. All things Western are available, and the fashions are both beautiful and fun (although fancy and pricey). They've even got home furnishings.

Saba's Western Stores. 7254 Main St., Scottsdale. ☎ **480/949-7404.**

Since 1927, this store has been outfitting Scottsdale's cowboys and cowgirls, visiting dude ranchers, and anyone else who wants to adopt the look of the Wild West. Call for other locations around Phoenix.

✪ **Sheplers Western Wear.** 9201 N. 29th Ave. ☎ **602/870-8085.**

Although it isn't the largest Western-wear store in the valley, Sheplers is still sort of a department store of cowboy duds. If you can't find it here, it just ain't available in these parts. Other locations include 8979 E. Indian Bend Rd., Scottsdale (☎ **480/948-1933**); 2643 E. Broadway Rd., Mesa (☎ **480/827-8244**); and 2700 W. Baseline Rd., Tempe (☎ **602/438-7400**).

Stockman's Cowboy & Southwestern Wear. 23587 N. Scottsdale Rd. (at the corner of Pinnacle Peak Rd.), Scottsdale. ☎ **480/585-6142.**

This is one of the oldest Western-wear businesses in the valley, although the store is now housed in a modern shopping plaza. You'll find swirly skirts for cowboy dancing, denim jackets, suede coats, and flashy cowboy shirts. Prices are reasonable and quality is high.

Women's Wear

In addition to the shops mentioned below, there are many excellent shops in malls all over the city. Favorite spots for upscale fashions include Biltmore Fashion Park, the ✪ Borgata of Scottsdale, ✪ El Pedregal Festival Marketplace, and Scottsdale Fashion Square. See "Malls & Shopping Centers," below for details on these malls and shopping plazas.

Carol Dolighan. At the Borgata, 6166 N. Scottsdale Rd., Scottsdale. ☎ **480/922-0616.**

The hand-painted, handwoven, and handmade dresses, skirts, and blouses here abound in rich colors. Each is unique. There's another Carol Dolighan store in El Pedregal Festival Marketplace, 34505 N. Scottsdale Rd. (☎ **480/488-4505**) in Carefree.

Objects. 7051 Fifth Ave., Scottsdale. ☎ **480/994-4720.**

This eclectic shop carries hand-painted, wearable art both casual and dressy, unique artist-made jewelry, African masks and Indian art, books, and all kinds of delightful and unusual things.

Uh Oh. In Hilton Village, 6137 N. Scottsdale Rd., Scottsdale. ☎ **480/991-1618.**

You'll find simple, tasteful, and oh-so-elegant fashions, footwear, jewelry, and accessories. The Southwestern contemporary styling makes this a great place to pick up something to be seen in. A second store is in La Mirada shopping plaza, 8900 E. Pinnacle Peak Rd., Scottsdale (☎ **480/515-0203**).

GIFTS & SOUVENIRS

One of the best places to shop for souvenirs is the Arizona Center mall in downtown Phoenix. See "Malls & Shopping Centers," below for details.

✪ **Bischoff's Shades of the West.** 7247 Main St., Scottsdale. ☎ **480/945-3289.**

This is one-stop shopping for all things Southwestern. From T-shirts to regional foodstuffs, this sprawling store has it all. It's got a good selection of candles, chile garlands (*ristras*), and wrought-iron cabinet hardware that can give your kitchen a Western look, and Mexican crafts that all fit in with a Southwest interior decor.

A GOLF SHOP

✪ **In Celebration of Golf.** 7001 N. Scottsdale Rd., Suite 172, Scottsdale. ☎ **480/951-4444.**

Sort of a supermarket for golfers (with a touch of Disneyland thrown in), this amazing store sells everything from clubs and golf shoes to golf art and golf antiques. There are even unique golf cars on display in case you want to take to the greens in a custom car. A golf simulation room allows you to test out new clubs and get in a bit of video golfing at the same time. An old club-maker's workbench, complete with talking mannequin, makes a visit to this shop educational as well as a lot of fun.

JEWELRY

Jewelry by Gauthier. 4211 N. Marshall Way, Scottsdale. ☎ **888/411-3232** or 480/941-1707.

This store sells the designs of the phenomenally talented jewelry designer Scott Gauthier. Very stylish, modern designs using precious stones make every piece of jewelry in this shop a miniature work of art. This is the only place you'll see Gauthier's work for sale in the United States. The elegant shop features a lit-from-below green onyx floor.

Molina Fine Jewelers. 3134 E. Camelback Rd. ☎ **800/257-2695** or 602/955-2055.

While you don't have to have an appointment to shop at this very exclusive jewelry store, it's highly recommended. With an appointment, you'll get personalized service as you peruse the Tiffany exclusives and high-end European jewelry. If you can spend as much on a necklace as you can on a Mercedes, this is where to shop for your baubles.

MALLS & SHOPPING CENTERS

Arizona Center. Van Buren St. and Third St. ☎ **480/949-4FUN.**

With its gardens and fountains, this modern downtown shopping center is both a peaceful oasis amid downtown's asphalt and a great place to shop for Arizona souvenirs (check out the Arizona Highways Gift Shop). Arizona Center is also home to several nightclubs and some of downtown's best restaurants.

Biltmore Fashion Park. E. Camelback Rd. and 24th St. ☎ **602/955-8400.**

With its garden courtyards and upscale boutiques, this open-air shopping plaza is *the* place to be if shopping is your obsession and you keep your wallet full of platinum cards. Shops bear the names of international designers and exclusive boutiques such as Polo, Gucci, Laura Ashley, and Cole-Haan. Saks Fifth Avenue and Macy's are the two anchors. There are also more than a dozen moderately priced restaurants here, and valet parking is available.

✪ **The Borgata of Scottsdale.** 6166 N. Scottsdale Rd. ☎ **480/998-1822.**

Designed to resemble a medieval Italian village complete with turrets, stone walls, and ramparts, the Borgata is far and away the most architecturally interesting shopping mall in the valley. There are about 50 upscale boutiques, art galleries, and restaurants here.

✪ **El Pedregal Festival Marketplace.** 34505 N. Scottsdale Rd., Carefree. ☎ **480/488-1072.**

Located adjacent to The Boulders resort 30 minutes north of Old Scottsdale, El Pedregal is the most self-consciously

Ten Fun Ways to Blow $100 (More or Less) in the Valley of the Sun

With greens fees for 18 holes of golf as high as $240, it is obvious that the Valley of the Sun is not exactly a cheap place for a vacation. Still, if you've budgeted plenty of money for your vacation or simply want to splurge on a memorable experience, there are quite a few great ways to blow 100 bucks while in town. Here are some of our favorites.

1. **Spend a day at a spa.** It's not often you can blow 100 bucks and come away feeling good about it, but for between $90 and $105, you can spend the day at one of the valley's resort spas getting pampered and de-stressed. You can also spend quite a bit more than $100 in a day, but can you really put a price on well being? See "Day Spas" earlier in this chapter.
2. **Rent a Vette** (☎ **480/941-3001**). Sometimes you just have to go over budget. For $149 a day, you can rent a new Corvette from Rent-a-Vette and head out for a high-speed spin in the desert or just cruise around Scottsdale looking like you belong.
3. **Hire a stretch limo for a couple of hours.** For $110 (plus a mandatory 20% gratuity for the driver) you can rent a six-passenger stretch limo from Arizona Limousines (☎ **800/678-0033** or 602/267-7097) for 2 hours. Just ride around, or maybe have the limo take you to a resort for a cocktail. Unfortunately, there's a 3-hour minimum on weekends, which would cost you $165 plus tip.
4. **Play a round of golf on an Arizona legend.** If you can get a tee time, $100 will get you a twilight round of golf on the Gold Course at the Wigwam Resort (☎ **623/935-3811**) out west in Litchfield Park. This is one of the oldest and most famous courses in the valley.
5. **Rent a cabana at the Pointe Hilton Tapatio Cliffs Resort** (☎ **602/866-7500**). If you've got a Motel 6 vacation budget but long for the resort life, why not rent a poolside

Southwestern shopping center in the valley. It's worth the long drive out here just to see the neo–Santa Fe architecture and colorful accents. The shops offer high-end merchandise, fashions, and art. The Heard Museum also has a branch here.

cabana at this north Phoenix resort? The cabanas go for $95 a day and are located in the resort's aquatic playground known as The Falls. Sure it would be cheaper to go to Big Surf, but the experience just wouldn't be the same.

6. **Take a hot-air balloon ride.** There is no better way to see the desert than drifting above it at dawn in a hot-air balloon, and there's just about no cheaper way in the country to take to the air than in the oldest form of flying machine. For $90 to $140, you can get airborne. See "Organized Tours & Excursions," earlier in this chapter.
7. **Take a hummer of a back-roads tour.** Why ride in a Jeep when you can ride in a Hummer, the ultimate off-road vehicle? For $90 to $100, Desert Storm Hummer Tours (☎ **480/922-0020**) will give you a ride to remember, and you'll get an up-close and personal look at the Arizona desert.
8. **Order the seasonal tasting menu at Mary Elaine's** (☎ **480/423-2530**). If you've never had a $100 dinner, maybe now is the time to indulge. How else will you ever be able to call yourself a true gourmand? This six-course dinner will set you back $110 (not including tax, tip, wine, or the cost of proper dining attire).
9. **Go on a C-note shopping spree at Biltmore Fashion Park.** Maybe $100 won't buy much at this boutique-filled upscale shopping plaza, but the fun of it can be trying to find the best $100 buy in the mall. Now there's a challenge to keep a shopaholic busy for the afternoon.
10. **Take a glider ride.** Sure, it sounds tame (there isn't even an engine), but opt for an aerobatic flight ($110) at Turf Soaring School (☎ **602/439-3621**) and you'll get a good idea of what it's like to be top gun. Loops and inverted flying make it clear that getting high in Arizona is a load of fun.

Scottsdale Fashion Square. 7014–590 E. Camelback Rd. (at Scottsdale Rd.), Scottsdale. ☎ **480/941-2140.**

Scottsdale has long been the valley's shopping Mecca, and for years this huge mall has been the reason why. It now houses five major department stores—Nordstrom, Dillard's, Neiman Marcus, Robinsons-May, and Sears—and smaller stores such as Eddie Bauer, J. Crew, and Louis Vuitton.

NATIVE AMERICAN ARTS, CRAFTS & JEWELRY

✪ **Bischoff's Shades of the West.** 3925 N. Brown St., Scottsdale. ☎ **480/946-6155.**

This museum-like store and gallery is affiliated with another nearby Bischoff's (see above, under "Gifts & Souvenirs"). However, here you'll find higher-end jewelry, Western-style home furnishings and clothing, ceramics, books and music with a regional theme, and contemporary paintings.

Faust Gallery. 7103 E. Main St., Scottsdale. ☎ **480/946-6345.**

Old Native American baskets and pottery, as well as old and new Navajo rugs are the specialties at this interesting shop. The gallery also sells Native American and Southwest art, including ceramics, colorful paintings, bronzes, home furnishings, and unusual sculptures.

Gilbert Ortega Museum Gallery. 3925 N. Scottsdale Rd. ☎ **480/990-1808.**

You'll find Gilbert Ortega shops all over the valley (including several in Old Scottsdale), but this is the biggest and best. As the name implies, there are museum displays throughout the store. Cases full of jewelry are the main attraction here, but there are also baskets, sculptures, pottery, rugs, paintings, and kachinas. Other branches are located at 7237 E. Main St., Scottsdale (☎ **480/481-0788**); at Koshari I in the Borgata, 6166 N. Scottsdale Rd., Scottsdale (☎ **480/998-9699**); at the Hyatt Regency Hotel, 122 N. Second St., Phoenix (☎ **602/265-9923**), and at Scottsdale Fashion Square (☎ **480/423-5818**).

✪ **Heard Museum Gift Shop.** In the Heard Museum, 2301 N. Central Ave. ☎ **602/252-8344.**

The Heard Museum (see "Discovering the Desert and Its Native Cultures" earlier in this chapter) has an awesome collection of very aesthetic, extremely well-crafted, and very expensive Native American jewelry, art, and crafts of all kinds. Fortunately, because the store doesn't have to charge sales tax, you'll save a bit of money. This is the best place in the valley to shop for Native American arts and crafts; you can be absolutely assured of the quality.

✪ **John C. Hill Antique Indian Art.** 6962 E. First Ave., Scottsdale. ☎ **480/946-2910.**

This store is for collectors and has one of the finest selections of Navajo rugs in the valley, including quite a few older ones. There are also kachinas, superb Navajo and Zuni silver-and-turquoise jewelry, baskets, and pottery. This shop sells only the highest quality items, so you can familiarize yourself with what the best looks like.

Old Territorial Shop. 7220 E. Main St., Scottsdale. ☎ **480/945-5432.**

This is the oldest Indian arts-and-crafts store on Main Street and offers good values on a large selection of jewelry, sand paintings, concha belts, kachinas, fetishes, pottery, and Navajo rugs.

OUTLET MALLS & DISCOUNT SHOPPING

Arizona Mills. 5000 Arizona Mills Circle, Tempe. ☎ **480/491-9700.** From I-10, take the Baseline Rd. east exit. From AZ 60, exit Priest Dr. south.

This huge shopping mall in Tempe is on the cutting edge when it comes to shop-o-tainment. Not only will you find lots of name-brand outlets, but you'll also find a big video arcade and an IMAX theater. With nearly ¾ mile of sensory bombardment, it might be a good idea to bring earplugs and walking shoes.

Last Chance. 1919 E. Camelback Rd. ☎ **602/248-2843.**

This is it, the last chance for men's and women's clothes and shoes. If it doesn't sell here, it's headed south of the border where they sell clothes by the pound. If ever there were such a thing as combat shopping, you'd find it here. The clothes are unbelievably cheap, but are often damaged goods (returns and such), so be sure to inspect every article closely before committing.

My Sister's Closet. 6206 N. Scottsdale Rd., Scottsdale (near Trader Joes). ☎ **480/443-4575.**

This is where the crème de la crème of Scottsdale's used clothing comes to be resold. You'll find such labels as Armani, Donna Karan, and Calvin Klein. Prices are pretty reasonable, too. Also at **Town & Country** shopping plaza at 20th Street and Camelback Road, Phoenix (☎ **602/954-6080**).

Wigwam Outlet Stores. 1400 N. Litchfield Rd. ☎ **623/935-9730.** Take the Litchfield Rd. exit off I-10.

If you're headed west from Phoenix and need a shopping break, you'll likely find some good deals at this outlet mall near the famous Wigwam resort. Bass, Bugle Boy, Harry & David, Mikasa, and Levi's are just some of the many stores.

7

Phoenix & Scottsdale After Dark

If you're looking for nightlife in the Valley of the Sun, you won't have to look hard, but you may have to drive quite a ways. Although much of the valley's nightlife scene is centered on Old Scottsdale, Tempe's Mill Avenue, and downtown Phoenix, you'll find things going on all over.

The best place to look for nightlife listings is in the *Phoenix New Times,* a weekly newspaper that tends to have the most comprehensive listings. This is also the publication to check for club listings and schedules of rock concerts at various concert halls. *The Rep Entertainment Guide,* published by *The Arizona Republic,* is another good place to look for listings of upcoming events and performances, although you won't find as many club listings as in the *New Times. The Rep* is included in the Thursday edition of the paper but is also distributed free of charge from designated newspaper boxes on sidewalks around the Valley. *Get Out,* published by the *Tribune,* is another similar tabloid format arts-and-entertainment publication that is available free and can be found around Scottsdale and Tempe. Other publications to check for abbreviated listings are *Valley Guide Quarterly, Key to the Valley, Where Phoenix/Scottsdale,* and *Quick Guide Arizona,* all of which are free and can usually be found at hotels and resorts.

Tickets to many concerts, theater performances, and sporting events are available through **Ticketmaster** (☎ **480/784-4444;** www.ticketmaster.com), which has outlets at Wherehouse Records, Tower Records, and Robinsons-May department stores. Tickets are also available at all **ETM/Dillard's** department store box offices (☎ **800/638-4253** or 480/503-5555).

1 The Club & Music Scene

The Valley of the Sun has a very diverse club and music scene that's spread out across the length and breadth of the valley. However, there are a few concentrations of clubs and bars (downtown Scottsdale, Tempe's Mill Avenue, downtown Phoenix).

With at least three sports bars, as many regular bars, a massive multiplex movie theater, and half a dozen restaurants, downtown Phoenix's **Arizona Center** is a veritable entertainment mecca. Within a few blocks of this mega-entertainment complex, you'll also find Phoenix Symphony Hall, the Herberger Theater Center, and several sports bars. However, much of the action revolves around games and concerts at the America West Arena and the Bank One Ballpark (BOB).

Another place to wander around until you hear your favorite type of music is **Mill Avenue** in Tempe. Because Tempe is a college town, there are plenty of clubs and bars on this short stretch of road.

In **Scottsdale,** you'll find an eclectic array of clubs in the neighborhoods surrounding the corner of Camelback Road and Scottsdale Road (especially along Stetson Drive, which is divided into two sections east and west of Scottsdale Road). This is where the wealthy (and the wannabes) come to party, and you'll see lots of limos pulling up in front of the hot spot of the moment (currently Axis/Radius).

As we're sure you know if you're a denizen of any urban club scene, nightclubs come and go. If you're interested in finding out what's hot, check the *New Times* for ads of places that play your kind of music. Many dance clubs in the Phoenix area are open only on weekends, so be sure to check what night the doors will be open. Bars and clubs are allowed to serve alcohol until 1am.

COUNTRY

✪ **Handlebar-J.** 7116 E. Becker Lane, Scottsdale. ☎ **480/948-0110.** No cover–$3.

We're not saying that this Scottsdale landmark is a genuine cowboy bar, but cowpokes do make this one of their stops when they come in from the ranch. You'll hear live git-down two-steppin' 7 nights a week and free dance lessons Wednesday, Thursday, and Sunday.

The Rockin' Horse Saloon. 7316 E. Stetson Dr., Scottsdale. ☎ **480/949-0992.** Cover varies from $5 to $50.

Located in the heart of Scottsdale, the Rockin' Horse is an ever-popular bar that books the best of local and national country acts.

Rusty Spur Saloon. 7245 E. Main St. (Old Scottsdale). ☎ **480/941-2628.**

A small, rowdy, drinkin' and dancin' place frequented by tourists, this bar is a lot of fun, with peanut shells all over the floor, dollar bills stapled to the walls, and the occasional live act in the afternoon or evening.

ROCK & R&B

The Bash on Ash. 230 W. 5th St., Tempe. ☎ **480/966-8200** or 480/966-5600. Cover $2–$21.

Located in downtown Tempe, this small club is the Valley's main swing-dance club. There are lessons and live bands several nights a week.

✪ **Cajun House.** 7117 E. 3rd Ave., Scottsdale. ☎ **480/945-5150.** Cover $5–$13.50.

The interior of this cavernous dance club is done up as a New Orleans street scene with doors opening into various bars, dining rooms, and lounges. Lots of fun and well worth checking out.

BLUES

Char's Has the Blues. 4631 N. 7th Ave. ☎ **602/230-0205.** No cover–$6.

Yes, indeed, Char's does have those mean-and-dirty, lowdown blues, and if you want them too, this is where you head in Phoenix. All the best blues brothers and sisters from around the city and around the country make the scene. You'll find this club 4 blocks south of Camelback Road.

The Rhythm Room. 1019 E. Indian School Rd. ☎ **602/265-4842.** No cover–$15.

This blues club, long the valley's most popular, books quite a few national acts as well as the best of the local scene, and has a dance floor if you want to move to the beat.

JAZZ

Orbit Restaurant & Jazz Club. In Uptown Plaza, Central Ave. and Camelback Rd. ☎ **602/265-2354.** No cover (2-drink minimum if you're not having dinner).

Big and trendy, this space has a very urban feel to it, which is surprising considering its shopping plaza location. Orbit is one of the most popular jazz clubs in the valley, although the music line-up sometimes includes blues and Motown.

✪ **Timothy's.** 6335 N. 16th St. ☎ **602/277-7634.** No cover.

This is the valley's top upscale jazz spot and attracts a well-off crowd. There's live jazz nightly, performed by the house band or touring combos. Timothy's is hard to beat when you're looking for an elegant, romantic evening of dining and listening to lively jazz.

COMEDY & CABARET

The Tempe Improv. 930 E. University Dr., Tempe. ☎ **480/921-9877.** Cover $12–$15 plus 2-item minimum.

With the best of the national comedy circuit harassing the crowds and rattling off one-liners, the Improv is the valley's most popular comedy club. Dinner is served and reservations are advised.

DANCE CLUBS & DISCOS

✪ **Axis/Radius Nightclubs.** 7340 E. Indian Plaza, Scottsdale. ☎ **480/970-1112.** Cover $5–$10.

If you're looking to do a bit of celebrity spotting, Axis is the place. Currently Scottsdale's hottest dance club and liveliest singles scene, this two-story glass box is a boldly contemporary space with an awesome sound system. You'll find this bar 2 blocks east of Scottsdale Road and 1 block south of Camelback.

Buzz Original Funbar. Southeast corner of Scottsdale Rd. and Shea Blvd. ☎ **480/991-FUNN.** No cover–$7.

In Scottsdale, folks like to think big. The resorts are big, the houses are big, the cars are big, the restaurants are big, and the nightclubs are big. Buzz boasts three different theme areas, including the Rat Pack Lounge, the Rhino Room (with a zebra-striped dance floor), and a patio up on the roof.

Club Rio. 430 N. Scottsdale Rd., Tempe. ☎ **480/894-0533.** Cover $5.

Popular primarily with students from ASU, which is just across the Tempe Town Lake, this club has a dance floor big enough for football practice. Music is primarily Top 40, alternative, and retro music, and there are also plenty of live shows.

Pepin. 7363 Scottsdale Mall, Scottsdale. ☎ **480/990-9026.** Cover $8.

A DJ plays Latin dance music from 10pm on Friday and Saturday at this small Spanish restaurant located on the Scottsdale Mall. Thursday through Saturday evenings, there are live flamenco performances.

Phoenix Live! at Arizona Center. 455 N. 3rd St. ☎ **602/252-2502.** No cover–$5.

Located on the second floor of the Arizona Center shopping center in downtown Phoenix, this trio of clubs (a piano bar, a dance club, and a sports bar) provides enough options to keep almost any group of bar hoppers happy. Also in Arizona Center, you'll find Moondoggie's, a beach-theme bar.

Sanctuary. 7340 E. Shoeman Lane, Scottsdale. ☎ **480/970-5000.** Cover $5–$10.

As the newest hot club in downtown Scottsdale, Sanctuary has raised the bar for high-end dance clubs. As with other area mega-clubs, there are different theme rooms, including a Moroccan room. Plenty of great martinis.

2 The Bar, Lounge & Pub Scene

AZ88. 7353 Scottsdale Mall, Scottsdale. ☎ **480/994-5576.**

Located across the park from the Scottsdale Center for the Arts, this sophisticated bar/restaurant has a cool ambience that's just right for a martini before or after a performance. There's also a great patio area.

Bandersnatch Brew Pub. 125 E. 5th St., Tempe. ☎ **480/966-4438.**

With good house brews and a big patio in back, Bandersnatch is a favorite of those unusual ASU students who prefer quality to quantity when it's beer-drinking time. There's live Celtic music Wednesday through Saturday nights.

Durant's. 2611 N. Central Ave. ☎ **602/264-5967.**

In business for decades, Durant's has long been downtown Phoenix's favorite after-work watering hole. Through wine coolers, light beers, and microbrews, Durant's has remained true to the martini and other classic cocktails.

The Famous Door. 7419 Indian Plaza, Scottsdale. ☎ **480/970-1945.**

Scottsdale's ultimate cigar bar, The Famous Door affects a Rat Pack aesthetic and treats cigars with reverence. Plenty of different martinis are available for accompaniment.

Hops! Bistro & Brewery. Scottsdale Fashion Square, 7014 E. Camelback Rd. ☎ **480/946-1272.**

Take a down-home idea—brewing your own beer—and mix it up with a bit of Phoenix chic (by way of San Diego) and you get Hops!, a huge, upscale brew pub with a boldly contemporary dining room that serves creative American cuisine.

✪ **Hyatt Regency Scottsdale Lobby Bar.** 7500 E. Doubletree Ranch Rd., Scottsdale. ☎ **480/991-3388.**

The open-air lounge just below the main lobby of this posh Scottsdale resort sets a romantic stage for nightly live music (often by Spanish guitarist Estéban). Wood fires burn in patio fire pits, and the terraced gardens offer plenty of dark spots for a bit of romance.

The Squaw Peak Bar. In the Arizona Biltmore Resort & Spa, 24th St. and Missouri Ave. ☎ **602/955-6600.**

Even if you can't afford the lap of luxury, at least you can pull up a comfortable chair in the lounge of the luxurious Arizona Biltmore. Sink into a seat next to the one you love and watch the sunset test its color palate on Squaw Peak. Alternatively, you can slide into a seat near the piano and let the waves of mellow jazz wash over you.

T. Cook's. 5200 E. Camelback Rd. ☎ **602/808-0766.**

Even if you aren't planning on having dinner at this opulent Mediterranean restaurant, you'll certainly enjoy lounging in the bar. With its mix of Spanish colonial and '50s tropical furnishings, this is as romantic a lounge as you'll find anywhere in the valley. For even more romance, snuggle up out on the patio by the fireplace

Thirsty Camel. At The Phoenician, 6000 E. Camelback Rd. ☎ **480/423-2530.**

Whether you've made your millions or are still working your way up the corporate ladder, you owe it to yourself to spend a little time in lounging in the lap of luxury. You may never drink in more ostentatious surroundings than here at Charles Keating's Xanadu. The view's pretty good, too.

COCKTAILS WITH A VIEW

The Valley of the Sun has more than its fair share of spectacular views. Unfortunately, most of them are from expensive restaurants. All these restaurants have lounges, though, where for the price of a drink (and perhaps valet parking) you can sit back and ogle a crimson sunset and the purple mountains' majesty.

Your choices include **Different Pointe of View** at the Pointe Hilton Tapatio Cliffs Resort, **Rustler's Rooste** at the Pointe Hilton on South Mountain, and **Top of the Rock** at The Buttes. All these restaurants can be found in chapter 5, "Dining."

SPORTS BARS

Alice Cooper'stown. 101 E. Jackson St. ☎ **602/253-7337.** Most nights no cover; special shows up to $25.

Sports and rock mix it up at this downtown restaurant/bar run by, you guessed it, Alice Cooper. Lots of TVs (including an impressive wall of monitors) and lots of signed sports and rock memorabilia. The Bank One Ballpark is only a block away.

America's Original Sports Bar. 455 N. 3rd St. ☎ **602/252-2502.** No cover–$5.

Located in the Arizona Center, this huge sports bar (nearly an acre) is a sort of fun center for grown-ups. There's a huge back deck and innumerable TVs (a half dozen of which are giant-screen). There's even a Phoenix Sports Hall of Fame.

Majerle's Sports Grill. 24 N. 2nd St. ☎ **602/253-9004.**

If you're a Phoenix Suns fan, you won't want to miss this sports bar only a couple of blocks from the America West Arena where the Suns play. Suns memorabilia covers the walls.

McDuffy's. 230 W. 5th St., Tempe. ☎ **480/966-5600.**

With more than 60 TVs and nearly two dozen beers on tap, this sports bar is a favorite of Sun Devils fans.

GAY & LESBIAN BARS & DANCE CLUBS

✪ **Ain't Nobody's Business.** 3031 E. Indian School Rd. ☎ **602/224-9977.**

Located in a small shopping plaza, this is the city's most popular lesbian bar, with pool tables and a nonsmoking lounge. On weekends the dance floor is usually packed.

Amsterdam. 718 N. Central Ave. ☎ **602/258-6122.**

Just a few doors away from Crowbar, Amsterdam draws a crowd that prefers sipping martinis to tossing down beers. There's no sign outside—you just have to look carefully for the number.

Crowbar. 702 N. Central Ave. ☎ **602/258-8343.** Cover $8.

This downtown Phoenix club stays packed with sweaty bodies on weekends. The decor is sort of industrial Gothic, with lots of big candles dripping wax down faux stone pillars. The after-hours scene pulls in the underagers and goes on until 4am. Open Thursday through Sunday.

3 The Performing Arts

The performing-arts scene in the Valley of the Sun grows more robust with each passing year. Major performing-arts venues are scattered across the valley, so no matter where you happen to be staying, you're likely to find performances being held somewhere nearby. Downtown Phoenix claims the valley's greatest concentration of performance halls, including the Phoenix Symphony Hall, the Orpheum Theatre, and the Herberger Theater Center. You'll also find large performance halls in Scottsdale, Mesa, Tempe, Chandler, and Sun City.

Calling these venues home are the valley's major performance companies—the Phoenix Symphony, Scottsdale Symphony Orchestra, the Arizona Opera Company, Ballet Arizona, Center Dance Ensemble, the Actors Theatre of Phoenix, and the Arizona Theatre Company. Adding to the performances held by these companies are the wide variety of touring companies that make stops in the valley throughout the year. These national and international acts give the valley just the diversity of performers you would expect to find in a city of this size.

While you'll find box office phone numbers listed below, you can also purchase most performing-arts tickets through **Ticketmaster** (☎ **480/784-4444**) or **ETM/Dillard's Box Office** outlets (☎ **800/638-4253** or 480/503-5555), found in Dillard's department stores around the city. For tickets to sold-out shows, check with your hotel concierge if you are staying at a hotel that has a concierge. Or try **Western States Ticket Service** (☎ **602/254-3300**) or **Tickets Unlimited** (☎ **800/289-8497** or 602/840-2340).

MAJOR PERFORMING-ARTS CENTERS

Phoenix's premier performance venue is the **Phoenix Symphony Hall,** 225 E. Adams St. (☎ **602/262-7272**), which is home to the Phoenix Symphony and the Arizona Opera Company and also hosts other classical music performances, Broadway touring shows, and various other concerts and theatrical productions

The **Orpheum Theatre,** 203 W. Adams Street (☎ **602/262-7272**), a historic Spanish colonial baroque theater, was built in 1929 and at the time was considered the most luxurious theater west of the Mississippi. Today its ornately carved sandstone facade stands in striking contrast to the glass-and-steel City Hall building with which the theater shares a common wall. Today, the Orpheum is once again the most elegant performance hall in the valley, and if you have time for only one show while in town, try to make it here.

In Scottsdale, the **Scottsdale Center for the Arts,** 7380 E. Second St., Scottsdale (☎ **480/994-ARTS;** www.ScottsdaleArts.org), hosts a wide variety of performances and series ranging from alternative dance to classical music. This center seems to get the best of the touring performers who come through the valley.

The Frank Lloyd Wright–designed **Grady Gammage Memorial Auditorium,** Mill Avenue and Apache Boulevard, Tempe (☎ **480/965-3434**), on the Arizona State University campus, is at once massive and graceful. This 3,000-seat hall hosts everything from barbershop quartets to touring Broadway shows.

In Scottsdale, near the Borgata shopping center, you'll find **ASU's Kerr Cultural Center,** 6110 N. Scottsdale Rd. (☎ **480/965-5377**), a tiny venue in a historic home. This center offers up an eclectic season that includes music from around the world.

OUTDOOR VENUES

Given the weather, it should come as no surprise that Phoenicians like to go to performances under the stars.

The city's top outdoor venue is the **Blockbuster Desert Sky Pavilion** (☎ **602/254-7200**), located ½ mile north of I-10 between 79th and 83rd avenues. This 20,000-seat amphitheater is open year-round and hosts everything from Broadway musicals to rock concerts; tickets run about $10 to $70.

The **Mesa Amphitheater,** at the corner of University Drive and Center Road in Mesa (☎ **480/644-2567**), is a much smaller amphitheater that holds rock concerts throughout the summer and occasionally other times.

Throughout the year, the **Scottsdale Center for the Arts** (☎ **480/994-ARTS**) stages performances outdoors in the adjacent Scottsdale Amphitheater on the Scottsdale Civic Center Mall.

Outdoor concerts are also held at various parks and plazas around the valley during the warmer months of the year. Check local papers for listings of such events.

Two perennial favorites of valley residents take place in particularly attractive surroundings. The Music in the Garden concerts at the **Desert Botanical Garden,** 1201 N. Galvin Pkwy. (☎ **480/941-1225**), in Papago Park, are held on Sundays between September and March. The season always includes an eclectic array of musical styles. Tickets are $13.50 and include admission to the gardens. Sunday brunch is served for an additional charge. Way up in Carefree, the **El Pedregal Festival Marketplace** (☎ **480/488-1072**) stages jazz, blues, and rock concerts on Thursday evenings (7 to 9:30pm) from April through June and the month of September. Tickets are $5 to $10.

CLASSICAL MUSIC, OPERA & DANCE

The **Phoenix Symphony** (☎ **800/776-9080** or 602/495-1999), the Southwest's leading symphony orchestra, performs at the Phoenix Symphony Hall (tickets run $19 to $43), while the **Scottsdale Symphony Orchestra** (☎ **480/945-8071**) performs at the Scottsdale Center for the Arts (tickets go for $15 to $20).

Opera buffs may want to see what the **Arizona Opera Company** (☎ **602/266-7464;** www.azopera.com) has scheduled. This company stages up to five operas, both familiar and more obscure, each year and splits its time between Phoenix and Tucson (tickets cost $20 to $70). Performances are held in Phoenix Symphony Hall.

Ballet Arizona (☎ **602/381-1096**) performs at the Symphony Hall, the Orpheum, and the Herberger Theater Center and stages both classical and contemporary ballets (tickets run $16 to $48). The **Center Dance Ensemble** (☎ **602/252-8497**), the city's contemporary dance company, stages several productions a year (one during the Christmas holidays) at the Herberger Theater Center (tickets go for $18). Between September and March each year, **Southwest Arts & Entertainment** (☎ **602/482-6410**) brings acclaimed dance companies and music acts from around the world to Phoenix, with performances staged at various area venues (tickets range from about $7 to $45).

THEATER

With nearly a dozen professional companies and the same number of nonprofessional companies taking to the boards throughout the year, there is always some play being staged somewhere in the valley. So if you're a fan of live theater, check around. You're likely to find something to pique your interest.

The **Herberger Theater Center,** 222 E. Monroe St. (☎ **602/252-8497**), which is located downtown and vaguely resembles a Spanish colonial church, is the city's main hall for live theater. Its two Broadway-style theaters together host hundreds of performances each year, including productions by the **Actors Theatre of Phoenix (ATP)** and the **Arizona Theatre Company (ATC).** ATP tends to stage smaller, lesser-known off-Broadway–type works, with musicals, dramas, and comedies equally represented; tickets go for $19 to $33. ATC is the state theater company of Arizona and splits its performances between Phoenix and Tucson. Founded in 1967, the ATC is the major force on the Arizona thespian scene. Productions range from world premieres to recent Tony award-winners to classics. Tickets run $22 to $34. Also performing at the Herberger is the **Arizona Jewish Theatre Co.,** which stages plays by Jewish playwrights and with Jewish themes. Tickets range from $24.50 to $26.50.

The **Phoenix Theatre,** 100 E. McDowell Rd. (☎ **602/258-1974** or 602/254-2151), has been around for almost 80 years and stages a wide variety of productions; tickets are $25 to $27. If your interest lies in Broadway plays, see what the

Valley Broadway Series (☎ **480/965-3434**) has scheduled. The series, focusing mostly on comedies and musicals, is held at the Gammage Auditorium in Tempe; tickets cost about $29 to $49. The **Theater League** (☎ **602/ 952-2881**) is another series that brings in Broadway musicals. Performances are held in the Orpheum Theatre, and tickets cost about $33 to $40. Scottsdale's small **Stagebrush Theatre,** 7020 E. Second St. (☎ **480/990-7405**), is a community theater that stages tried-and-true comedies and musicals, with the occasional drama thrown in. Tickets are about $12 to $17. For more daring new works and children's theater, check the schedule at **PlayWright's Theatre,** 1121 N. First St. (☎ **602/ 253-5151**). Tickets are about $12.

4 Casinos

Casino Arizona. U.S. 101 and Indian Bend Rd. and U.S. 101 and McKellips Rd. ☎ **480/850-7777.**

These casinos are the newest and most conveniently located casinos in the area. They're both located just off U.S. 101 on the east side of Scottsdale and offer plenty of slot machines, cards, and other games of chance.

Fort McDowell Casino. On Fort McDowell Rd. off Ariz. 87, 2 miles northeast of Shea Blvd., Fountain Hills. ☎ **800/THE-FORT.**

Phoenicians, once among the mainstay clientele of casinos in Nevada, now need not even leave the valley to throw their hard-earned dollars at the slot machines and video-poker games.

Gila River Casino. Exit 162 off I-10 south of Phoenix. ☎ **800/WIN-GILA.**

With two separate casino buildings at the same exit off I-10, the Gila River Casino wants to make sure it snags some business from passing motorists. Keno, bingo, and slots machines are available.

Harrah's Phoenix Ak-Chin Casino. 15406 Maricopa Rd., Maricopa. ☎ **800/HARRAHS.**

Located 25 miles south of Phoenix and just south of the town of Maricopa, this glitzy casino on the Ak-Chin Indian Reservation brings Las Vegas–caliber gambling to the Phoenix area. Lots of slot machines, video poker, a card room, keno, and bingo. To reach the casino, take Exit 164 (Queen Creek Road) off I-10, turn right, and drive 17 miles to Maricopa.

8

Side Trips from Phoenix

If you have the time and inclination, there are many worthwhile attractions just outside of Phoenix. Within little more than an hour's scenic drive, you can explore ghost towns, Native American ruins, and innovative architecture—and do some golfing and shopping along the way.

1 The Apache Trail

There isn't a whole lot of desert or history left in Phoenix, but only an hour's drive to the east you'll find quite a bit of both. ✪ **The Apache Trail,** a winding, partially gravel road that snakes its way around the north side of the Superstition Mountains, offers some of the most scenic desert driving in central Arizona. Along the way are ghost towns and legends, saguaros and century plants, ancient ruins, and artificial lakes.

This tour includes a lot of driving on a narrow, winding gravel road, and if you'd rather leave the driving to someone else, you can take a tour of the area with **Apache Trail Tours** (☎ **480/982-7661**), which offers four-wheel-drive tours of different lengths ($60 to $125 per person), as well as hiking trips ($10 per person per hour with a 4-hour minimum) into the Superstition Mountains.

To start this drive, head east on U.S. 60 to the town of Apache Junction and then head north on Arizona 88. Just 3½ miles north of Apache Junction, you'll come to **Goldfield Ghost Town,** a reconstructed 1890s gold-mining town. Although it's a bit of a tourist trap—gift shops, an ice-cream parlor, and the like—it's also home to the **Superstition Mountain/Lost Dutchman Museum** (☎ **480/983-4888**), which has interesting exhibits about the history of the area. Of particular note is the exhibit on the Lost Dutchman gold mine, perhaps the most famous mine in the country despite the fact its location is unknown. Admission to the museum is $2 for adults, $1.50 for seniors, and 75¢ for children. **Goldfield Ghost Town and Mine Tours** (☎ **480/983-0333**) provides

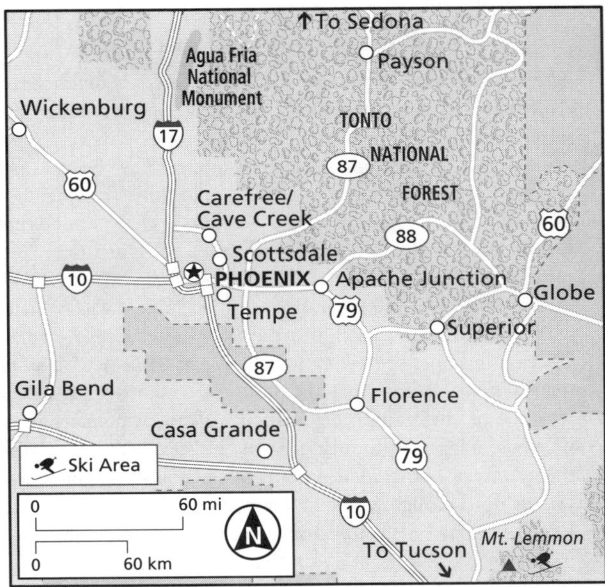

guided tours of the gold mine beneath the town ($5 for adults, $3 for children ages 6 to 12). The company also operates a narrow-gauge railroad train, which circles the town (rides are $4 for adults, $2 for children ages 5 to 12). If it's lunchtime already, you can get a meal at the steakhouse/saloon.

Not far from Goldfield is **Lost Dutchman State Park** (☎ **480/982-4485**), where you can hike into the rugged Superstition Mountains and see what the region's gold seekers have been up against. Park admission is $5 per vehicle, and there is a campground that charges $10 per site.

Continuing northeast, you'll next come to **Canyon Lake,** the first of three reservoirs you'll pass on this drive. The three lakes provide much of Phoenix's drinking water, without which the city would never have been able to grow as large as it is today. Here at Canyon Lake you can go for a swim or take a cruise on the ***Dolly*** **steamboat** (☎ **480/827-9144**). A 90-minute cruise on this reproduction paddle wheeler costs $14 for adults and $8 for children 6 to 12. Dinner cruises are also available. Or, for a taste of the Old West, hold out for **Tortilla Flat** (☎ **480/984-1776**), an old stagecoach stop that has

The Lost Dutchman of the Superstitions

The Superstition Mountains rise up to the east of Phoenix, dark and ominous, jagged and hot. Cacti bristle across the mountains' flanks, and water is almost nonexistent. Yet for more than a century, gold-crazed prospectors have been scouring these forbidding mountains for a gold mine that may not even exist. The power of a legend is strong, and few legends are as well documented as the legend of the Lost Dutchman gold mine.

The year was 1870 when two German miners, Jacob Waltz and Jacob Weiser, set off into the Arizona wilderness east of Phoenix in hopes of striking it rich. When these two "Dutchmen" (an appellation derived from the German word *Deutsch*) returned to civilization, they carried with them pouches filled with gold nuggets. Although unsavory prospectors tried to track them to their mother lode in hopes of claim jumping, none was successful. Through visits to saloons and brothels, the two Jacobs remained tight-lipped about their mine's whereabouts.

a restaurant, saloon, and general store, all of which are papered with business cards and more than $50,000 worth of dollar bills left by travelers who have stopped here. If it's a hot day, don't miss the prickly pear ice cream (guaranteed spineless).

A few miles past Tortilla Flat, the pavement ends and the truly spectacular desert scenery begins. Among the rocky ridges, arroyos, and canyons of this stretch of road, you'll see saguaro cacti and century plants (a type of agave that dies after sending up its 15-foot-tall flower stalk). Next you'll come to **Apache Lake,** which is in a deep canyon flanked by colorful cliffs and rugged rock formations. This lake also has a marina, as well as a campground, motel, restaurant, and general store.

Shortly before reaching pavement again, you'll reach **Theodore Roosevelt Dam.** This dam, built in 1911, forms Roosevelt Lake and is the largest masonry dam in the world.

Continuing on Arizona 88, you'll next come to ✪ **Tonto National Monument** (☎ **520/467-2241**), which preserves the southernmost cliff dwellings in Arizona. These pueblos were built between 1100 and 1400 by the Salado people, and are some of the few remaining traces of this tribe that once

Jacob Weiser eventually disappeared from the scene amid speculation that his partner did him in so as to keep all the gold to himself. Waltz eventually gave up prospecting in the Superstitions in 1889 at the age of 80. On his deathbed in 1891, he gave detailed directions to a Phoenix woman he had befriended. She and her foster son and the foster son's father and brother spent the next 40 years searching fruitlessly for Waltz's Lost Dutchman mine. Waltz's dying directions just weren't good enough to lead the searchers through these rugged, uncharted mountains.

Clues to the mine's location abound, and hopeful prospectors and treasure hunters have followed every possible lead in their quest for the mine. However, gold fever has led more than a few to their deaths in this harsh wilderness. While skeptics say that there's no proof there ever was a Lost Dutchman mine, others see in the mine's continued elusiveness hope that they might one day be the prospector to find this fabled mother lode.

cultivated lands now flooded by Roosevelt Lake. The lower ruins are ½ mile up a steep trail from the visitor center, and the upper ruins are a 3-mile round-trip hike from the visitor center. The lower ruins are open daily year-round except Christmas, and the upper ruins are open November through April by reservation (reserve at least a couple of weeks in advance). The park is open daily from 8am to 5pm (you must begin the lower ruin trail by 4pm), and admission is $4 per car.

Continuing on Arizona 88 will bring you to the copper-mining town of **Globe.** The mines here are open pits, and although you can't see the mines themselves, the tailings (remains of rock removed from the copper ore) can be seen piled high all around the town. In Globe, be sure to visit ✪ **Besh-Ba-Gowah Archaeological Park** (☎ **520/425-0320**), which is on the eastern outskirts of town (open daily 9am to 5pm; admission $3 for adults and $2 for seniors; children 12 and under are free). This Salado Indian pueblo site has been partially reconstructed, and several rooms are set up to reflect the way they might have looked when they were first occupied about 700 years ago. These are among the most fascinating ruins in the state. To reach Besh-Ba-Gowah, head out of Globe on South Broad Street to Jesse Hayes Road.

From Globe, head west on U.S. 60. On the west side of Superior, you'll come to ✪ **Boyce Thompson Southwestern Arboretum,** 37615 U.S. 60 (☎ **520/689-2811**), which is dedicated to researching and propagating desert plants and instilling in the public an appreciation for desert plants (open daily, except Christmas, 8am to 5pm; admission $5 adults and $2 children 5 to 12; free for children 4 and under). This was the nation's first botanical garden established in the desert, and the cactus gardens are impressive. The setting in Queen Creek and Anett canyons is quite dramatic with cliffs for a backdrop and a stream running through the gardens. As you hike the miles of nature trails, watch for the two bizarre boojum trees.

If after a long day on the road you're looking for a good place to eat, stop in at **Gold Canyon Golf Resort,** 6100 S. Kings Ranch Rd., Gold Canyon (☎ **480/982-9090**), which has a good formal dining room and a more casual bar and grill.

2 Cave Creek & the Old West

A drive north from Phoenix can give you glimpses into how the pioneers once lived—and how Hollywood imagines Western towns should look.

Head north out of Phoenix on I-17 for about 20 miles and take the Pioneer Road exit. Here you'll find the ✪ **Pioneer Arizona Living History Museum,** 3901 W. Pioneer Rd. (☎ **623/465-1052**). This museum includes nearly 30 original and reconstructed buildings, and on-site you'll find costumed interpreters practicing traditional frontier activities. There are also melodramas and gunfights staged daily. Among the buildings are a carpentry shop, a blacksmith shop, a miner's cabin, a stagecoach station, a one-room schoolhouse, an opera house, a church, farmhouses, and a Victorian mansion. The museum is open October through May, Wednesday to Sunday 9am to 5pm, and June through September, Friday to Sunday 5 to 9pm. Admission is $5.75 adults, $5.25 seniors and students, $4 children 6 to 12, and free for children under 4.

Heading back south on I-17, take Exit 223 and head east to **Cave Creek** and **Carefree.** Cave Creek, founded as a mining camp in the 1870s, clings to its Wild West image and looks something like the fake cow towns all over the Arizona desert. Carefree, on the other hand, is all New West retirees, mansions, and golf courses. To learn more about the history of this area, stop in at the **Cave Creek Museum** at the corner of Skyline Drive and Basin Road (☎ **480/488-2764**). The museum is open October through May, Wednesday to Sunday 1 to 4:30pm, and admission is by donation.

Cave Creek is home to several Western steakhouses, saloons, and shops selling Western and Native American crafts and antiques. When you've worked up a thirst or a hunger, wander over to **Crazy Ed's Satisfied Frog Saloon,** 6245 E. Cave Creek Rd. (☎ **480/488-3317**), where you can get some hearty Western fare and sample Cave Creek chile beer, each bottle of which has a whole chile pepper in it. For dining with a little more finesse, consider the **Tonto Bar & Grill,** 5734 E. Rancho Mañana Blvd. (☎ **480/488-0698**), which overlooks the Rancho Mañana golf course. Patio dining and a contemporary American menu make this place an inviting spot for a meal. Rancho Mañana Boulevard is at the west end of town just off Cave Creek Road; if you can, call for a reservation.

Carefree is a much more subdued place, a planned community established in the 1950s and popular with retirees. Ho Hum Road and Easy Street are just a couple of local street names that reflect the sedate nature of the town, which is home to the exclusive Boulders resort. Boasting one of the most spectacular settings of any resort in Arizona, The Boulders also has a couple of excellent restaurants.

On Easy Street, in what passes for downtown in Carefree, you'll find one of the world's largest sundials. The dial is 90 feet across, and the gnomon (the part that casts the shadow) is 35 feet tall. From the gnomon hangs a colored-glass star, and in the middle of the dial is a pool of water and a fountain. This elaborate timepiece shows the correct time on vernal and autumnal equinoxes, but on other days of the year, you have to consult a chart next to the sundial to determine the correct time.

In downtown Carefree, you'll also find a sort of reproduction Spanish village shopping area, and just south of town, adjacent to The Boulders resort, you'll find the upscale **El Pedregal Festival Marketplace** shopping center, where there are lots of interesting shops, art galleries, and a few restaurants.

If you'd like to do a bit of horseback riding while you're in the area, contact **Cave Creek Outfitters** (☎ **480/471-4635**), just off Dynamite Boulevard on 144th Street. They charge $55 to $65 for a 2-hour ride. There's also plenty of good mountain biking in the area, and if you'd like do a bit of fat-tire riding, you can rent a bike from **Cave Creek Bikes,** 6149 Cave Creek Rd.

3 South of Phoenix

Driving southeast from Phoenix on I-10 for about 60 miles will bring you to the Florence and Casa Grande area, where you can learn about Indian cultures both past and present and view the greatest concentration of historic buildings in Arizona.

To reach Florence, continue south on I-10 to Exit 185 (Ariz. 387) and head east. Before reaching Florence, near the town of Coolidge, you'll come to ✪ **Casa Grande Ruins National Monument** (☎ **520/723-3172**). In Spanish, the name means "Big House," and that's exactly what you'll find. In this instance, the big house is the ruin of an earth-walled structure built 650 years ago by the Hohokam people. Although it's still not known what purpose this unusual structure served, the building provides a glimpse of a style of ancient architecture rarely seen. Instead of using adobe bricks or stones, the people who built this structure used layers of hard-packed soil that have survived the ravages of the weather. The Hohokam people who once occupied this site began farming the valleys of the Gila and Salt rivers about 1,500 years ago, and eventually built an extensive network of irrigation canals for watering their fields. By the middle of the 15th century, however, the Hohokam had abandoned both their canals and their villages and disappeared without a trace. The monument is open daily 8am to 5pm (closed Christmas), and admission is $2 for adults.

Continuing east, you'll soon come to the farming community of **Florence.** Although at first glance this town may seem like any other small town, closer inspection turns up more than 150 buildings on the National Register of Historic Places. The majority of these buildings are constructed of adobe and were originally built in the Sonoran style, a style influenced by Spanish architectural ideas. Most buildings were altered over the years and now display aspects of various architectural styles popular during territorial days in Arizona.

Before touring the town, stop in at the **Pinal County Historical Society Museum,** 715 S. Main St. (☎ **520/868-4382**), to learn more about the history of the area. It's open Wednesday to Saturday 11am to 4pm and Sunday noon to 4pm (closed from mid-July through August). Admission is by donation.

At the corner of Main Street and Ruggles Street, you'll find the **McFarland State Historic Park** (☎ **520/868-5216**), which is housed in a former Pinal County Courthouse built in 1878. It's open Thursday to Monday 8am to 5pm; admission is $2 adults, $1 children ages 12 to 18. The current county courthouse, built in 1891, rises above the center of town and displays an unusual combination of different architectural styles.

To find out more about the buildings of Florence, stop in at the **Florence Visitors Center,** 291 N. Bailey St. (☎ **800/437-9433** or 520/868-9433), housed in a historic 1891 bakery in the center of town.

If you're interested in shopping deals, there are a couple of **factory-outlet shopping malls** in the town of Casa Grande at exits 194 and 198 off I-10. They are only a short distance out of your way to the south if you are headed back to Phoenix.

4 En Route to Northern Arizona

If your idea of a great afternoon is searching out deals at factory outlet stores, then you'll be in heaven at **Prime Outlets at New River,** 4250 W. Honda Bow Rd. (☎ **623/465-9500**). Among the stores here are Barneys, Ann Taylor, Bugle Boy, Gap, Geoffrey Beene, and Levi's. Take Exit 229 (Desert Hills Rd.) off I-17.

A little farther north, you'll find the town of Rock Springs, which is barely a wide spot in the road and is easily missed by drivers roaring up and down I-17. However, if you are a fan of pies, then *do not* miss Exit 242 off the Interstate. Here you'll find the **Rock Springs Cafe** (☎ **623/374-5794,** or 602/258-9065 in Phoenix), which has been in business since 1910. Although this aging nondescript building looks like the sort of place that would best be avoided, the packed parking lot says different. Why so popular? No, it's not the coffee or the "hogs in heat" barbecue or even the Bradshaw Mountain oysters. No, what keeps this place packed are Penny's pies, the most famous pies in Arizona (32,891 sold in 1998). No matter what your favorite type might be, you'll likely find it in the pie case. If one slice isn't enough, order a whole pie to go; you can enjoy it when your day's driving is over. As the menu says, this place is "worth the drive from anywhere."

If you have an interest in innovative architecture, don't miss the Cordes Junction exit (Exit 262) off I-17. Here you'll find ✪ **Arcosanti** (☎ **520/632-7135;** www.arcosanti.org), Italian architect Paolo Soleri's vision of the future—a "city" that merges architecture and ecology.

Soleri, who came to Arizona to study with Frank Lloyd Wright at Taliesin West, envisions a compact, energy-efficient city that disturbs the natural landscape as little as possible—and that's just what's rising out of the Arizona desert here at Arcosanti. The organic design of this city built of cast concrete will fascinate both students of architecture and those with only a passing interest in the discipline. Arcosanti has been built primarily with the help of students and volunteers who come and live here for various lengths of time.

To help finance the construction, Soleri designs and sells **wind-bells** cast in bronze or made of ceramic. These distinctive bells are available at the gift shop here.

If you'd like to stay overnight, there are basic accommodations ($30 to $75 double per night) available by reservation, but you must arrive before 5pm. You'll also find a bakery and cafe on the premises. Arcosanti is open daily 9am to 5pm, and **tours** are held hourly 10am to 4pm ($5 suggested donation).

Some 71,000 acres of land east of I-17 between Black Canyon City and Cordes Junction was, in early 2000, designated the **Agua Fria National Monument,** which is administered by the Bureau of Land Management, Phoenix Field Office, 2015 W. Deer Valley Rd., Phoenix, AZ 85027-2099 (☎ **623/580-5500**). The monument was created to protect the region's numerous prehistoric Native American ruin sites, which date from between A.D. 1250 and 1450 (at least 450 prehistoric sites are known to exist in this area). There is very limited access to the monument and no facilities for visitors. The only roads within the monument are rugged dirt roads, many of which require four-wheel-drive and high clearance.

Index

See also Accommodations and Restaurant indexes, below.

General Index

Phoenix Accommodations

Phoenix Restaurants

Scottsdale Accommodations

Scottsdale Restaurants